DISCLAIMER: This is a work of fiction and this statement is included to inform the reader that any celebrity name(s), business name(s), location(s), product(s), and organizations that are stated in the content of this book are real. However, they are used in a purely fictional way.

LOVE'S MIRAGE II

BY: MoniB

Love's Mirage II

By MoniB

Cover Illustrated by Isaac Brown

Cover Created by Jazzy Kitty Publications

Logo Designs by Andre M. Saunders/Jess Zimmerman

Editor: Anelda L. Attaway

© 2021 MoniB "Monica Betts"

ISBN 978-1-954425-33-0

Library of Congress Control Number: 2021919831

All rights reserved. This book is protected by the copyright laws of the United States of America. This book may not be copied or reprinted for commercial gain or profit. The use of short quotations or occasional page copying for personal or group study is permitted and encouraged. Permission will be granted upon request. This book is for Worldwide Distribution and printed in the United States of America, published by Jazzy Kitty Publications utilizing Microsoft Publishing Software. Please be advised this book has strong language and content. Parental Advisory is suggested due to mature content. Disclaimer: This is a work of fiction and that any celebrity name(s), business name(s), location(s), product(s), and organizations while real are used in a purely fictional way.

ACKNOWLEDGMENTS

First and foremost, I would like to God for His many blessings and ideas to keep you reading. Without Him, this book would not be.

Thank you to my mother and father, who have kept me uplifted with support.

Thanks to my siblings, all of y'all played your part in keeping me inspired and full of ideas for my next book.

Thank you, Jazzy Kitty Publications, Mrs. Anelda, you're truly wonderful.

Last but definitely not least, I would like to thank my readers. You all keep me motivated to keep writing and making new stories to tell. It's truly a blessing for your support.

I'm so excited to be able to present to you Love's Mirage II. It was fun writing it and be sure to keep a look out for the final book of the series Love's Mirage III.

TABLE OF CONTENTS

INTRODUCTION	i
CHAPTER ONE	01
CHAPTER TWO	21
CHAPTER THREE	37
CHAPTER FOUR	56
CHAPTER FIVE	73
CHAPTER SIX	97
CHAPTER SEVEN	123
CHAPTER EIGHT	144
CHAPTER NINE	168
ABOUT THE AUTHOR	193

INTRODUCTION

Join me in this continuation of Love's Mirage II.

Samone takes cover and tries to wait out all of the wrongs currently happening in her life. Charles is taking steps to keep Samone safe, but are they the right measures that should be taken? Samone reconnects with her father and tries to patch things up with her sister Dedra.

After getting word of Joshua's affairs, Charles heads to a meeting with all the kingpins in the area. He learns some vital information that will take him and Samone on a journey to Chicago.

I hope you, my reader, enjoyed the first book of Love's Mirage, and I'm so happy to present Love's Mirage II. I hope you enjoy it and keep a lookout for Love's Mirage III.

CHAPTER ONE

We were in the car on our way to Charles's place when the police flashed her lights for us to pull over and stop. Charles began to get nervous and uneasy. He began to fidget.

"Charles, what is the problem? Why are you acting like this?"

"Samone leave me alone."

"No, tell me, do we have something to worry about?"

Just as I was about to ask him if he had any marijuana in the car, the policewoman instructed Charles to roll down the window.

"Good evening, folks. I notice that one of your taillights is out. I need to see your license, registration, and proof of insurance, please."

Charles reached over and opened his glove department. He handed her the appropriate information and she said, "Sir, did you know that your taillight is out?"

"No, Ma'am. I didn't. It must have just went out today because the last thing I know about it is that it was fine."

I could tell Charles was nervous and I would be too if I were him, for he had a stash of marijuana in the glove department. It wasn't that much from what I saw, but it was there big as day.

"Alright, Sir, I will take your word on it. Let me go and run your license and I will be right back. If everything is okay, you and your wife can be on your way." Charles took the insurance card and registration from her and hurriedly put them in the glove department.

"Are you alright, Sir?" Charles looked toward the bright light that was peering in on us.

"Yes, I'm fine, Officer."

"Well, alright, but you seem nervous to me."

"Officer, I just have to go to the bathroom."

"Oh, okay. Well, let me go and check your status and I will be right back."

"Okay Officer." She turned and left to go to her car.

I was relieved because that bright light was killing my eyes.

"Just play it cool Charles. I don't feel like going to jail tonight."

"What are you talking about Samone?" We turned to both face each other.

"Boy please, you know what you got in that glove department. Don't play dumb." He turned his eyes to face the stirring wheel.

"I'm cool Samone. You heard her. If everything is alright with my license, then we are on our way."

"Well, is everything alright with it?"

"Yep. Just got through with all my legal issues." There was silence in the car as we waited for her to return.

"Alright, Sir, I saw that you just recently paid for a ticket that was issued earlier this year but other than that, everything is legit. I'm going to let you off with a warning. You really need to get that taillight fixed as soon as possible. The next officer won't be as generous as I am being. You are free to go. Get that taillight fixed and have a nice evening."

"Thank you, Officer." He retrieved his license and started the car.

He was about to put his car in drive when I reminded him to put on his blinker.

"Good thinking Samone." He pulled off and we were on our way again.

At first, there was silence, but I broke it with my opinion of what he should do with his life.

"Charles, you really need to give up that crap. I mean, we could have both been going to jail tonight behind that crap." He didn't say anything.

"Do you hear me? Hello. Earth to Charles."

"Yea, I hear ya… and don't tell me wat' to do. I aliedy' kno wat to do."

"Oh, do you now?"

"Yeah, so just back off me, a'ight!" I looked over to face him, but his eyes were on the road.

I realized that I was tired of fighting and arguing. My head was beginning to pound with excruciating pain, so I decided to lay off him.

"Charles, I'm sorry for prying in your business. Whatever you do is fine with me."

"That's all you gonna say? I'm expecting mor' than dat."

"I'm just tired of fighting and all the arguing. I'm just ready to lie down and rest. My head is really killing me right now."

"You know what, Samone?"

"What's that?"

"I love you. I really do. And if that bastard of a man come and try to harm you again, I will kill him."

The way the words rang in my ear let me know that this man was very serious. I thought it was just better if I didn't say anything. So, we sat there in silence for the duration of our trip.

When we made it to his home, it seemed as if he was expecting company, for his place was spotless. The Charles I knew didn't have an organized place, let alone a clean environment.

"Do you usually keep your place this clean now?"

"Um yeah, I do. Why are you so surprised?"

"Well, I haven't been over here in a while and I see that you have new furniture. Heck, everything is new. It looks like something out of a magazine."

"Thank you for da' compliment. I tried to make it look betta in here after we broke up."

I looked at him and he looked around the place like he was impressed with his own work. I know I was being paranoid when I had the thought that this could be someone else's place. When I was just about to ask him if it was, he turned to me with a huge smile. I smiled back.

"Why are you smiling so hard?"

"Oh, nothing."

"Uh-huh, sure. What is the smile about."

"Okay, ok. I guess I will spill the goods. I have something for you. Have a seat while I go and get it."

Charles left me to sit down and enjoy the cushion of a fairly new black leather couch. His couch almost felt as good as mine did. I looked around one more time and found pictures of him on the walls. One of which stood out the most. It was when he and I were dating. We were all smiles and in love in that picture. I didn't find another female besides myself hanging on the wall (other than family). I found myself smiling with satisfaction at that fact. In some kind of twisted way, I was thrilled at the fact that I still had Charles wrapped around my finger. But don't get it twisted; I have mad love for him as well. I mean, he is here by my side when it seems like everyone else has turned their back on me. My sister was angry at the fact that her man wanted me and not her. She pretended that the real reason was because of the kiss. But trust me, I know my sister. And then there is my sweet dear mother. Yeah, right, she would take Dedra's side any day over me. It seemed like she detested me when I made Dedra upset. Dedra was her sweet little angle that could do no wrong. She doesn't know Dedra like I knew her. The fact that she lied to my mother about her virginity and not caring if there was a God or not… leaves me to wonder what else she has lied to my mother about. But hey, I'm the bad seed. Oh well. I exhaled and closed my eyes while leaning back into the couch. While my eyes were shut, I felt a presence in the room. It was Charles trying to sneak back in without disturbing me. Suddenly, I heard some soft jazz music playing from the speakers that were on the wall.

"Mmmm… Billie Holiday."

I opened my eyes to find Charles in a dark shimmered silk robe and pants set. He stood over me, smiling with those deep cutthroat dimples. Dimples that were to die for. I couldn't take my eyes off him. He looked so desirable, but to be honest, I wasn't in the mood. My head was still throbbing, but I wasn't going to tell him that.

"So, since when did you start listening to Billie Holiday?" He handed me a glass of champagne off of the tray that he was holding.

"Since you romanced me that night. Do you remember this attire?"

While he was still standing, I looked up from the glass and found his eyes piercing down upon me, waiting for me to speak. We locked eyes and we engaged in a conversation. Not with words but that of the eye.

"Of course, I remember that intoxicating piece that I bought for you. You know what? You still look good in it. Is this the surprise that you spoke of?"

"Somewhat. There is more that follows. Please, Ms. Gray, just relax and enjoy this special event that I have planned just for you."

He left me in silence to only beckon for me to join him in the bathroom moments later. The thoughts that began to race in my head jolted my emotions for him. My emotions then began to erase all the thoughts that I had going on. I had become a human pin doll that was feeling everything. I was feeling happy, loved, and overbearing peace. I enjoyed these feelings bundled up into one. I entered the bathroom to find rose petals scattered everywhere and the tub was filled with bubbles. I couldn't help but notice Stevie Wonder's Make Sure You Are Sure song on the stereo. Charles really surprised me with this. I wasn't expecting to be wined and caressed with such love and care.

"All I really want to do is make you feel better before you went to sleep. I know that it is really late and you are probably ready for bed, but I wanted to surprise you."

I walked over to Charles and put my index finger on his lips, and said, "Ssshh.

It is quite alright. I'm thankful to have such a person like you in my life."

"I'm not sure if you would like for me to bathe you or if you wanted to do that yourself... but I'm more than willing to do the job." I pushed him back to the toilet for him to take a seat.

"How about I undress and you do the honors of washing me." He smiled with satisfaction that his plan to seduce me was working.

I stepped into the water, which to my surprise, was just right. From my experience with men, I found that they like the temperature a little less hot than we women do. Charles walked over to the tub and reached for the soap and towel. He then kneeled and began to cover my backside with soap. He cleansed it with such ease and gentleness. No one ever had the pleasure, the notion, to bathe me. I felt so honored and special. He loved me, this man in front of me. As nothing was being said, I smiled at the present. The time that we were in was pleasant, comfortable, and non-wavering.

"I agree dis is nice," Charles replied to my speechless thoughts.

It wasn't before long that I was finally clean. He stood and grabbed the towel that was hanging on the door. I stood in the tub, naked as can be, when he looked at me with kind eyes that displayed love and not lust, as Joshua usually did.

"Please, would you wipe me down, for I am beginning to be chilled by the air?"

"I'm sorry."

He walked to where I was standing and began to wipe me down with even strokes. With the towel around my torso, I stepped out of the tub. He grabbed me by my shoulder and turned me around to face him. Charles landed a soft kiss upon my lips that it startled me. I couldn't remember the last time I felt so adored. My emotions caused my aching head to become something of the past. I was now in the mood.

"Samone, you make me moan..." he whispered.

I giggled softly like a schoolgirl who just found out that the boy she liked equally felt the same way for her.

"What is it?"

"I want to take a moment out of life and create a long-lasting description of what I feel... and what I desire in mind... which is to love you in any way imaginable. I want to create a life with you. I desire to know what life would be to have someone to hold on to at night."

While looking into his eyes, I felt a lightning bolt strike me in my soul. It moved me to see what he saw in his eyes. I saw me.

He took me by the hand and led me to the bedroom. He embraced me with kisses that were necessary for me to recuperate from seeing the past, present and future all at once when I looked in his eyes. I feared that I would disappoint him in a mortifying way. I wanted to share a life with him as well. Great things come to those who wait patiently, I thought to myself. I've been patient, I've prayed, I've trusted, I've fought the battle of dealing with lies from a different situation. Surely, this must be it. My soul mate has finally found me. Things began to intense and felt me with passion and love that would undeniably change my life.

"Charles, would you believe me when I say that you are the one for me to be with for life?"

"Yes, Samone. I believe you."

He entered my soul, he challenged my thoughts to stay, and he instilled in me a lesson to be learned. He began to say soothing words in my ear that I had never witnessed him to say. Then he parted my legs and worshipped me with thrusts of love. He became my moon and stars that were laid upon me to witness.

I thought to myself, *"Why haven't I experienced this thing before with Joshua. He has been my love for years now and this feeling this vision has never happened before. A greater lover Charles proved to be that night. My thoughts were his and his were mine."*

We shared Heaven that night. Our bodies lie on the bed while our souls become one within itself, a rapture. After our time of intimacy, we descended from heaven and lay there breathing heavily. Not a word was spoken, but there were many thoughts meant to be said.

I couldn't imagine being with anyone else that appeared in my life after this night. There was no question in my mind that it was Charles Lucas Brown that would be my lover and friend. He was my true love made and designed as pacifically for me as I was for him. Dedra was going to have to forgive me, for it is Charles that I want. I hated the fact that my sister was still upset with me. She knew the truth that Charles intended to marry me. She knew more secrets of him than me, for I could tell. It was not my problem that Brian wanted me. My dear sweet sister, she will have to realize that I'm not the blame for the mishap. All the facts were explained and I would have to leave it at that.

At that moment, my mind eased itself into a mode of freedom from thought. It escaped to a place that I hadn't truly been for in a while; it reached its limit though I wasn't finished. I slept so peacefully despite my restless nights. I dreamed a dream that involved Charles and me. It was pleasant and had mischief in it. Just as I was about to learn the moral of the dream, I felt a kiss on my forehead.

"I love you Samone Gray."

"I love you too."

He was surprised to learn that I was awake, for he hesitated and replied, "I thought I was in a dream with you tonight. I never experienced the lovemaking and blissful affection that you gave to me. I was taken to a place that I did not think I would ever see or feel. Could you believe that?"

"Oh, Charles. I feel the same way. I want to have someone to hold and have for all the rest of my natural life."

"Well, you have me. I will not leave your side in any way. You have my soul and heart; don't misuse them, take care of them. In doing this, I will, in return and do the same for you. Let's make a promise." I opened my eyes to find him looking at me with a fixation of solitude.

"What is that you care to say, Charles?"

"Let's marry. I want to be the one whom you hold at night. I prefer to be the man who will be your knight in armor." He gently graced my face with the touch of ease caress.

"Charles. I would like for you to be sure of this thing that you have proposed. I have a lot of problems in my life right now. A lot of which you know, but there is some that I haven't desired to share with anyone because of the insufficient confidence it has left me with."

"Are you referrin' to your medical condition?" Somewhat shocked by his accuracy, led me to believe that there was nothing he did not know about me.

"Can you tell me what it is?"

"Yes, I can. It deals with your mind. Am I right?"

History told its tale of him and me regarding my life. I consoled in him the truth, "Yes, My Love, it is. How did you know?"

"Remember when you dropped your prescription? Well, I looked at the name of the medication and then followed up with information about it. Turns out it is a chemical for the mind."

Impressed with the will of this man, the infatuation or love for me, the thoughtfulness he bestowed on me gave me the great idea that he was always protecting me in the hour of my need.

"Great, are you to do such things to learn about my shortcomings. Yes, you are correct."

There was silence. Enough time to let the other think about what was said. Charles directed the silence by interrupting it, "I don't mind your shortcomings, for they are what make you." Never knowing what he would say or do left me anxious to know him even more.

"Could you hold me closer?"

He pulled me closer to his body. I instantly felt safe and secure in his passionate arms. Nothing else was said, but we drifted off to sleep. The romance of the early morning ended with such peace.

When we woke up, I studied his face. It was very soothing and tactful to the point where I kissed it.

"Good day, My Love."

"You are so radiant and beautiful. And I am well aware of what I have requested of you. So, do me the honor of loving me till I die."

"My Love, I will." He jumped from the bed with such a spin it startled me at first.

"Come join me." After agreeing to be his help-mate, I followed his lead and jumped out of bed with the same thrill and joy.

We danced and moved with no music. The world became still and everything went into slow motion. He had the biggest smile showing the dimples that I truly envied for myself. We were touched by a mysterious feeling that we know to be from God. We were touched with a feeling of perfect happiness, joyous joy, and perfect peace. We danced till we got breathless, for we were excited about the future and how we were going to be together. If anyone were to have seen us dancing so, would have thought of us to be crazy, but very skilled. On the bed now, we were facing each other, breathing heavily.

"Oh wow, I didn't know you could move like that. Where did you pick up such skills?"

I beamed with satisfaction that he noticed my art, "I love to dance. It's good for the soul."

"You are so right about that." With that, he disappeared into the bathroom and came back out with a charismatic smile.

As he led his steps to me, having something behind his back, he said, "Are you ready for a surprise?"

I gleamed with delight and then answered, "Of course."

He put a small jewelry box in my hand and exclaimed, "I was intending on giving this to you last night with the official proposal, but I got carried away with the built-up emotions. I hope you forgive me. Open it."

Like a child waiting to be praised with a gift of satisfaction, he smiled anxiously. I opened the boxed and it beholds the most beautiful diamond I had ever seen. It was tiffany cut styled with the face of a man and woman side by side imprinted upon it. I was able to see the detail of the man's face and found it to be Charles, and the woman was me.

"Wow, Charles, you have really outdone yourself with this. This is a work of art." It was a nice-sized diamond, for I was able to see myself in it so clearly.

"What made you do this?"

Charles looked at me as if he were trying to read my thoughts. I didn't give him the reaction that he wanted, I presumed.

"You don't like it do you?"

A tear fell from my eye; it was the most thoughtful and great expression of love that has ever been offered to me. I looked at Charles, who had turned his head out of confusion.

"Charles. Look at me." He did as I asked.

"This is by far the best-given gift that I have ever received in my life. You put a lot of thought in this, for this is quite unique. I have never known anyone to do this. I'm grateful to have someone like you in my life." I embraced his face with warm kisses that I delivered from my heart.

"There's no stopping us Samone. The world is made for us to be a witness of love and endure it to the fulfillment of God. So cherish me as I will do the same for you. You have no idea how much love and respect that I have for you. Last night you told me that you had problems. Problems of which I'm sure I can handle. You are my heart and now you will be my life." My heart began to race with such speed that I was afraid I wouldn't be able to stop it.

"Charles. I will forever love you. I desired of such romance and now I find that God has answered my prayers with you. I don't know why I didn't see this tenderness and sweetness that you have displayed upon me in the twinkling of an eye."

I assured him that I loved the treasure of purity that caused me to be moved. I took the ring out of the box and allowed him to place it upon my finger. It was perfect.

"Let's never fight Samone. Let's always talk about our problems...." The song 'Let's Stay Together' played by Al Green as Charles went to the living room to answer his cell phone. I set on the bed admiring my ring and realized that it was a perfect fit without mentioning my ring size to Charles.

How could I behold a love like this? This was like a fairy-tale love, a dream to approach with ease for the fear that it would erupt. I waited patiently for Charles to return, but he did not. It was so quiet and I feared the worst. I got up from the bed and went into the living room to find my fiancé sitting on the couch with his head in his hands. I rushed over to his aid.

"What's wrong?"

He didn't respond. Instead, he looked at me with tears in his eyes.

"It's your mother."

I gasped for air and tried to breathe, but I could not. I tried to ask what happened, but no words were heard.

Seeing that I was in trouble, Charles came to my rescue and said, "Breath Samone. Breath."

He demonstrated the action of taking deep breaths. I did as instructed and to my surprise, it worked.

"Charles, what in the world are you talking about? My mother? What's going on?"

"Well…," he turned his head out of discomfort. I turned it back to me.

"Well what?"

He took a deep breath and proceeded to tell me that Joshua was seen with her last and that no one had seen her since. I got up from the couch and began to pace my steps. I thought horrible thoughts. I was scared, frightened that something had happened to my mother.

"Charles, what am I to do? I can't just let this happen…."

Charles stood and walked over with open arms to take my pain away. I cried and cried some more.

"There. There. Samone com' on, we are gonna see what we can do about this." I let him take the lead and was led to the bedroom.

"Put on your clothes Samone. Stop standing there." Not hearing what he was saying, I began to have some thoughts about what was going on.

"What did Joshua want with my mother," I thought.

I began to dress and Charles was finished and waiting on me. Great things come to those who wait... This was the second time I had this thought. It had meaning. It was moving.

"Charles, maybe we should just wait."

"Wait for what? This is your mother we are talking about."

"Charles, honestly, what can we do?"

"We can find Joshua and then we can find your mother."

"I think I need to handle this on my own. It's me that Joshua wants."

"Goodness Samone, what are you talking about?"

"Well, he is a drug lord and the last time I saw him, he walked out of my room at the hospital without telling me where he was going. I'm afraid he is performing on his anger of finding out the mishap with Brian. I'm sure he didn't take it good."

"Do you really think he will hurt your mother?"

I looked at him with solitude tears falling from my eyes, "I really don't know Charles. I hope not. God knows, I hope not."

"Great. Now we have some psycho on the loose with Denise. Your mother is now my mother and we have to get her back. Forget the cops...." He walked over to me and placed his hands on my shoulders.

"I know I am asking a lot of you to do this, but in order to get her back, you have to call Joshua and see what he wants. Do you think you can handle that?"

I quivered with such fear but answered him with a whisper, "Yes."

"Good." He left me for a second and came back with my cell phone.

"Okay. Now sit down and take your time but call him and see what the hell is going on." Looking bleak in my movements, Charles ushered me to the bed.

"I don't know Charles. What if something has happened to her already? What will I do with myself?"

"There is no time to worry about that. She is fine. We just need to find her as soon as possible."

I noticed the control of the situation that Charles had over me. He was very thoughtful and precise on what we should do. I watched him lead and direct this ordeal with the willingness to gain some strength and build my composure. I dialed the number. The phone rang four times before he answered it.

"So, now you decide to call. Since when did it take so long for you to get back at me?"

"Joshua. Have you seen my mother?"

"Straight to the point, huh, Samone? I like that."

"Have you seen her?"

"Maybe."

His voice was so cold and calm that it was quite scary. I didn't know how to react to his sudden reaction over the kiss.

"What is it Joshua? What do you mean maybe?"

I tried to keep my voice cool and calm, but I was very bad at it. Joshua knew that I was upset and he took advantage of my dismay.

"Do you want to see your mother again?"

"Of course. Where is she? Is she harmed in any way?"

"Look, I didn't want to do this, but some circumstances have come up. All they want… I mean, all I want is for you to meet me at the Chili's where we had dinner that night."

I wonder what he meant by they. I knew it was more to it. And then it hit me like when a deer is stuck in a daze of headlights. He was speaking of Tyrone and Michelle. I knew it had to be them.

"Who else would want me," I thought to myself.

Someone was going to have to handle Michelle and Tyrone. They are messing around with family now. My mother has nothing to do with the animosity that we share.

"Sure Joshua, I will meet you. What time?"

"Oh, let's say about 45 minutes from now. And Samone, don't bring anyone with you."

Why was he telling me not to bring anyone? I studied the silence that he gave me and I heard my mother. She was trying to tell me something, but that's when the phone went dead. I could just imagine my mother tied up while looking for someone to rescue her.

"So, what did he say?" I looked at Charles, who watched me close my phone and inhaled air into my lungs.

"He said to meet him at Chili's and to come alone in 45 minutes."

"Well, you know that is definitely out of the question. I'm not letting you go anywhere by yourself." I was about to argue with Charles but decided not to.

When we made it to Chili's, I noticed that the money green Lexus was in the parking lot, empty. Knowing who it belonged to made me wonder if

I could still trust that person. A part of me still wanted to, but I knew that I couldn't. Things were too strange and it was evident that I was a victim. While waiting in the car, Charles came up with a plan.

"Ok, this is what's going down. You go in and I will follow you after a while. Don't look for me, for he will suspect something is up. A lot of people are around, so he shouldn't try to do anything to you. If you get scared, just get up and leave. We will then contact the police to handle this situation."

I was so nervous; my hands began to shake. I had this eerie feeling that something was going on with Joshua. I had a lot of questions flowing within me.

"Joshua has something going on and I can't put my finger on it, Charles." Our eyes met and he saw the fear that was within mine.

"I know, I was thinking the same thing. It's kind of strange for him to meet you at a place like this. If it were me, I would want privacy. Give me that ring. I don't want him to lose his cool off of it." I looked down at my ring that I had forgotten I had on.

"You are right. Good thinking." I took the fancy ring off and handed it to him.

"Okay Baby, I think it's about time for you to go. Remember, I'm here."

"Okay." We kissed and he told me that he loved me.

"I love you too."

I opened the door and then a feeling of urgency came upon me. Let your will be done, Lord, I silently prayed. I walked into the entrance to find Joshua still standing in the front with the hostess.

"My party has finally made it, Ma'am," he said while looking at me.

I couldn't control my fidgety hands or my slow step. The hostess led the way to a table that was in the far back of the restaurant. I took the seat that faced the door. I didn't want Joshua to see Charles when he entered through the door.

"Joshua, where is my mother?"

"Don't worry, she is safe. I have her with a couple of friends."

"What? Are you crazy? Why did you take my mother?"

"We took your mother because we wanted you to suffer." He let out a horrendous laugh that had some of Chili's customers look our way.

"Hey, I know you two. You were here the other day," Kimberley said, beaming at us. Her facial expression soon changed when we didn't smile back.

"Well, can I get you anything?"

Joshua turned his head to greet the young Kimberley and replied, "Yes, I'll have a glass of water. Do you want anything, Dear?"

"No, I'm fine."

I was too anxious to know about my mother that I had lost all appetite and need for beverages. I became furious and something took over my tongue.

"Look, Joshua. If something should happen to my mother, you are going to be in a heap of trouble.

"I can't imagine you doing anything to me Samone. Stop playing around with threats, for it is not your style."

"If you hurt my mother, I will have someone murder you. This is not a threat. This is a guarantee."

"Ooo...aren't we tough. I still have no fear of you. Matter of fact, you couldn't even muster up the desire to see me suffer. I have you where I want you."

"No, you don't. You see, I came up with something the day you told me to use my brain. And I have. So, you should fear what is coming to you."

Joshua became uneasy in his seat. I could tell that he wanted to know what I had up my sleeve because he started to look around the room.

"Who do you have here with you?"

"Do you really think I'm going to tell you my secrets? You are surprising me with your actions on this day. I didn't expect you, of all people, to do me this way. You changed. I hate you."

"Remember, I still have your mother. So, you can hate me all you want. You can make plans…do whatever it is you need to do. I'm not afraid."

"You know what? Your threats have not scared me either. I will have my mother returned unto me. If my mother is not within my care in the next three hours, you are a dead man." With that, I stood and I gathered my composure to walk out. As I was exiting the door, Charles came in.

"So, you have this weakling helping you. You are going to need more than him to finish me," Joshua said, passing me on my way out. He took out a gun and showed it to Charles.

"This is what you will need to finish me. Your girlfriend here has put a threat on my life. Bring it on."

He pushed past Charles and hurriedly took steps to his car. We rushed out and Charles yelled after him.

"You better believe I can bring it. Trust that."

Joshua turned his head to see us walking to Charles's car. He was soon in his car and he drove off.

CHAPTER TWO

We watched Joshua drive out of the parking lot then Charles said something to me.

"Samone, we don't have to worry about those S.O.B.'s right now. I got a surprise for you in the car. I looked at him, confused.

"Charles, what are you talking about? My mother needs us." We arrived at the car and he motioned for me to look in the car.

"What do you see, My Dear?"

"Mama!" I yelled.

"Baby, I'm so glad to see y'all. I thought I was going to die." I looked from my mother to Charles back to my mother.

"Charles, where was she?"

"I found her in the trunk of that crazy fool's car…." I hugged my mother and all three of us got into the car. "…When you were in there… I started praying for you and your mother." Charles cranked up the car and began to drive.

"Something told me to look in the trunk. I got my tools and popped the trunk and there she was."

"Charles, you are something else. I know who intervenes on our behalf. It was God," I announced.

"Baby, you are so right about that. God has all control over everything. I was doing a lot of praying myself… mostly for you. They had me in a dark room full of storage items. I heard them talk about you like a dog. That crazy girl Michelle… told Joshua about Charles and he went berserk. I thought they were going to kill me, but Tyrone kept saying that they needed me alive for leverage. Thank God Charles found me." We were on I-35 headed to

Charles's place; I exhaled and gave thanks to God.

"It was me they wanted," I said, ending the silence that had built.

"Why? What do they want?"

"Joshua said that they wanted me to suffer." Charles looked at me and back at the road.

"Why do they want you so bad? What did you do?"

"Well, that's what I was trying to figure out. I have done nothing. It has to be something that they want from me. I know…"

"What is it Baby?" my mother asked.

"They want that money that I have. That's the only thing that I can come up with."

"Money? What money?" Charles asked.

"Well, a while back, Joshua gave me some to put away from him. He made me swear that I wouldn't tell him where it was until the big deal arrived."

"What have you done? You have put us all in danger. You have to give it back Samone," cried my mother.

"I will Mother, but I can't right now. If I did or we did, I looked at Charles… we may end up losing our lives."

After that, no one said anything else until we made it to Charles's place and my mother was impressed.

"You have a nice place Charles."

"Mama, have you ever met Charles before?"

"Yes, I have. Dedra brought him over to the house one day. He is such a nice young man."

"I know Mama, he is." Charles looked us over and a small smile appeared. He looked to be in much thought, though.

So, I asked him, "What is it Charles? What's wrong?"

"Well, I have a lot on my mind. I'm trying to figure out how I'm going to take care of Joshua and his latest crew. I know he will be looking for us as soon as he finds out that he doesn't have his leverage anymore."

Charles sat down on the couch and looked to the ceiling… "Lord, I know you hear me. Please help me with this situation as well."

"Why don't y'all just call the police."

"Well, I would, but I don't know who Joshua is paying off. I remember him telling me that he pays off judges and policemen too." My mother couldn't believe what she was hearing.

"Samone, did you really think that it would have lasted?" My mother was now sitting by Charles, rubbing his back to try to soothe all the troubles away.

"Mama, I have no words to express the magnitude of my dismay. I can't answer your question, for I truly don't know how to answer it. He showed a different side to me and not the side he is today."

"Dedra! Call her right now, Samone," Charles almost yelled. I was so relieved to have my mother back that I forgot about my sister.

"Charles, she is not answering my calls. You or mama is going to have to call her."

"Fine." He took out his cell phone and dialed my sister's number.

"Dedra, thank God. Leave your job now. Go to Brian's or the cops. Joshua and his crew are on the hunt for trouble. Yes, your mother is fine. She is here with us. No, you can't come over here… we are about to leave," he paused for a moment and then answered her with, "be careful, and we will meet you at the station. Okay. Leave now. Bye."

"I take it she is okay?"

"Yes," he sighed with relief. She's fine."

"So, what now?" asked my concerned mother?"

Charles turned his attention to me, "Samone, what did you say to Joshua?" He said in a way that led me to believe that he was worried and outdone with the activities that were taking place.

"Charles. Something came over me and I told him that if you hurt my mother that I would have someone murder him. That it wasn't a threat but a promise. He didn't believe me, though."

"Why would you say such nonsense Samone?" asked my mother. I scratched my head and looked away.

"Mother, I had no choice but to try and make Joshua believe that I was capable of doing something dangerous to him. I had a reason to do so, for you are my mother and I wanted you back."

"Well, now we have to prepare for war. I'm ready." Charles stood up and looked at his watch.

"I think it's time to take you to the police station, Mrs. Gray. No one will give thought to go into a police department and capture you again."

"Are you okay with that Mama?"

"Yes, Baby. Take me where I will be safe. I don't want to be in harm's way again. What do you mean you ready Charles? I hope you are not planning on doing anything crazy."

"Mrs. Gray, I do apologize for breaking this news to you this way, but I asked Samone to marry me and she agreed." My mother gasped.

"Oh my, what a surprise! But what does that have to do with what you are planning on doing?"

"Well, she is my responsibility now. I must take care of her and the things that come up dealing with her." My mother smiled with approval.

"Well, let's go."

We arrived at the Austin Police Department at 4:30 p.m. I knew that it would be busy, but I had no clue as to how many policemen and policewomen there would be. It was a grand building that consisted of computers, fax machines, and telephones. It had everything that a much-approved office should have, except there were not enough desks for each officer. For the short time that we waited for the clerk to help us, I studied the movement of the atmosphere. People were going to and fro, shuffling paper, clicking the keys on the keyboard, and reviewing monitors. One officer was hitting and cursing at a copier as if it would help the situation.

"Can I help you Ms.?"

I turned my head to face a brown-haired woman that had an artificial smile upon her face. She was about my size but taller and she had green eyes. I thought she was pretty if she would have had her hair hanging down.

"Yes Ma'am. We are here to speak to Captain Haynes."

She looked me over and announced, "Well, he is currently busy right now. Is there someone else that I can get for you?"

"No, he is the only person that can help me right now. He already knows me and my situation." Just then, the Captain walked by us with his eyes on paperwork.

"Captain Haynes. Captain Haynes."

He looked up from his reading and said, "Oh, hi there. I was wondering when you were going to contact me. It's great to see you up and about. The last time I saw you… you were in the hospital getting stitches."

"Are you here to help me still?"

"Of course! Let's go to my office and talk more." We followed his lead to his office and I noticed a smirk on the clerk's face as I passed her desk.

"Have a good day Ma'am."

"Thank you, officer. You do the same."

We made it to Captain Haynes's office and realized that he was a very busy man. He had loads of case files everywhere and many awards hanging on the wall.

"Oh uh… I wasn't expecting company. Let me clear some of this mess out of the way." He moved files to the floor and placed more on his oak and brass desk.

"Please sit."

"Captain Haynes, I would like to introduce you to my mother, Denise Gray, and my fiancé Charles Brown. They are here for help as well."

"So, what has changed your mind about receiving help from us?"

"Well, there is this man name Joshua Franks… and this crazy girl named Michelle," my mother looked at me and then motioned for me to finish her thoughts, "well, Captain Haynes. When Joshua Franks took my mother, I was sore afraid of what would happen to her. She was without blame in the situation, but they took her to get to me."

"Who are they?" Captain Haynes looked to Charles, who then began to speak.

"Michelle Carlbright, Tyrone Green, and Joshua Franks: those are the three that we think took her, Denise that is."

"Okay, so where can I find the people that you have named?"

"That, we do not know right now Captain, but we do know that we have made them more avenged than ever." Captain Haynes leaned back in his seat and studied our faces.

"Oh really, how so?"

"Well…" Charles looked at me with such sharp eyes that I stopped before I finished.

"Captain Haynes."

He took the tip of the pen from his mouth and answered Charles, "Yes, Mr. Brown."

"How do we know that you are safe to talk to?" His blue eyes seemed to turn a shade of red with anger.

"What are you insinuating?" He was very cruel, with a calmness that it was hard to embrace.

"Because the word on the streets is some judicial folks are being paid to assist."

My lover and friend were so diverse than any man I have encountered. He didn't trust too many people. He asked the questions that I would have never thought to answer. My heart began to ache with such lust for his thoughts. I wanted to be on the same page. I looked at Charles, finding him sitting on the edge of his seat, daring the Captain to lie to him.

"How dare you come in my office and challenge my authority? I have no reason to deal with scumbags out there in the streets."

"How should we determine the truth?" The Captain was leaning on his desk with both elbows supporting his weight.

"You just have to. You will have to believe me."

"Why is that?" I asked. Both men looked at me as I distracted the fumes of anger.

"Have you any nerve to ask me such questions?" My mother sat in her chair with beads of sweat from the heated conversations.

"I wonder. Why would he lie to us y'all? He is the Captain and besides that, we have nowhere else to go." My mother was right.

Charles began to ease back in his seat and said, "Well, I just wanted to make sure that this man is legit. I still have my doubts." Seeing the concern that Charles displayed, the Captain took it upon himself to prove himself accountable and trustworthy.

"Young man, there is no doubt to be left for you have after I share this with you." Captain Haynes pulled open his drawer and pulled out a tape recorder.

"I have conversations of two people shared over the phone. A friendly contact of mine gave it to me to investigate. I would like for you to listen and tell me if you could witness the voices that are on here."

"Baby...," I heard Michelle say, "...we are gonna be the ones who will take control over Joshua's empire. No one will be able to come between us. Just stick to the plan and we can succeed with swiftness."

The reluctance that I heard in Tyrone's voice touched me, "I want you. I want to have all the things that Joshua has, but I wish there were another way that we could do this."

"Look, we only have a couple of weeks before the big drop goes down and we need to get that money from Joshua. So, suck up your loyalty to him and do this for us."

"I know you want this and I do too, but maybe we should leave out Samone and her family."

"Uugh... you are beginning to get on my nerves. I told you if Joshua gets in our way, we will kill her. We will only do this if we can't get our hands on that money."

I was so clueless to her, Michelle, the girl that became a sister to me. I looked at the Captain and he was sitting in disgust. He shook his head and looked at me with concern. I didn't want him to see the fear in my eyes, so I turned my face. He knew exactly what I was doing and he turned the recorder off.

"I promise you. If I were paid by anyone... I wouldn't be sharing this evidence with you." I guess that was enough to convince Charles, for he stood up and gave me a hug.

"You don't have to worry about anything Ms. Gray. The Austin Police Department is at your service."

I was grateful to hear such words, but for some reason, I felt that it wasn't enough. I admired the ambition and determination the Captain had to find the creeps that were threatening lives.

"Thank you, Captain Haynes, but I have a favor to ask of you."

"What is it? Anything you name it," the Captain asked while standing?

"I would like for you to keep an eye on Denise for me. I think that they are trying to capture Samone's family to scare her."

"Sure. I can arrange that. I will have a policeman escort her to a hotel. No one will know where she is. What about Ms. Gray?"

Charles looked at the Captain and announced that he and I should leave the city. Charles also expressed his gratitude. We then exited the door. Captain Haynes was fearful for my life, so he rejected the thought of us leaving on our own.

He yelled behind us, "Mr. Brown, I do believe you are making a mistake. Come back. Let's reason together." Charles and I kept walking as if we did not hear the remarks of the Captain.

I had a clue what Charles was planning to do, so I went along with things. I believe that he would protect me and keep me from harm.

"Charles, what are we going to do?"

We were going 75 on the highway. Charles glared out at the road with rage in his eyes. I wanted to try to calm him down, but I did not know what to say.

"Charles." He didn't answer me until we pulled up to a house on MLK.

The house was surrounded by gangsters, hoodlums, and tramps-looking females. It was like a scene off the movies.

"Charles, what are we doing here? Who lives here?"

"Don't worry about it Samone. Just get out of the car and don't say a word." I exhaled.

I didn't know what exactly was going to go down, but I had a feeling that it was going to affect me in the worse way. Inside the house, it consisted of dirty furniture and a carpet that appeared to have been a red wine color but was now black with dirt.

"Hey, y'all look who popped up?"

I peered at the 6'5 Latino male. He had a piercing in his nose and was also placed upon his left eyebrow. He looked to be really scary, for he had tattoos of dragons and skulls that were very detailed. I looked away, for we almost caught eyes.

"So, homs'…who is dis'?"

"Chico, I need to talk to you. Is there somewhere we can talk?"

"Of course. You know mi casa is tu casa. Follow me." Charles turned to me and initially tried to have me sit down and wait.

"No, Charles. I want to go with you," I whispered. He gave me a hug of assurance that everything would be okay.

"Trust me Samone; no one is going to hurt you here. They are all in my debt for something I did for them a long time ago," he whispered back. His smiles of dimples smooth the rough edges of fear from my mind.

"What did you do?"

"Sssh...I can't tell you that right now. Later." We entered the dimmed lit room to find Chico already sitting.

"Hey, I thought you were gonna tell her to stay in da' other room."

"Nah, she's with me, Chico, all the way. Samone, here, needs to know what I'm planning to do."

Chico shrugged his shoulders and said, "Alright homs' whatever...," he turned his face to look at mine, "...but I hope you don't scare easy. I'm afraid we do work around here that don't suit yo' kind." We all looked at each other for a minute before Chico finally broke the silence.

"So, what is it that you want CB?"

Chico became a different character in an instant. He became less aggressive. Chico folded his hands on the table, but I could tell he was signaling for the hoodlums outside the window to go away.

"I see you haven't changed a bit Chico."

"I see that you have," Chico said, glancing at me. Charles slid his hand in mine and announced his engagement with me.

"Samone, congratulations. You have a good man on yo' arm," Chico said convincingly.

"Great are your words, Chico."

"Well, I like to think so…Chico," I proudly announced.

"Let's move on the next subject."

"Well, Chico it's like this. I know you have been itching to get revenge on Joshua Franks. Well, now your chances have come up."

I listened to the conversation and realized that Charles had kept Joshua alive for me. Everyone in that house wanted Joshua dead for what he did to their leader in past years.

"So, that's what you want us to do?"

"Yes. Can you finish the job?"

"Of course, homs'."

I heard things that I would rather not have learned. Charles was quite ruthless. From what happened early this morning, it was hard to accept that Charles was just as bad as Joshua. He believed that what he had planned would work. Only we will have to wait and see.

A week had passed and everything was still following its course. I wasn't sure if Michelle or Tyrone would still be hunting for me at my apartment, but we took the chance to go over anyway. Once we arrived, we noticed that the door was unlocked and opened. No one was there, but there was an enormous amount of damage done to my belongings. My couches were spray painted with profanity. The bedroom had urine stains on the floor. Also, my mattress was stabbed with a knife. The only thing that seemed to still be in order was my clothes. For some apparent reason, the devious and outrageous lunatics left me to be appreciative of the gesture.

"I knew this was going to happen," Charles said as he skewed his face.

"Charles, this is my life work here. Everything that I own is now gone,"

I said, dismayed.

"Baby, don't worry about it. I have you covered."

"I know you do, but I did this. This wasn't given to me. I worked so hard at making my place a nice one."

Charles didn't say another word but just listened, which was good because I just wanted to vent to someone. I found a letter written by someone other than the perpetrators we originally suspected. It read: *I had your mother, but you took her away from me. Now I have destroyed what you loved most. Just give up the money, or we will make your life a living hell. Don't get it twisted; I still have you where I want you. Signed, Who Cares.* As I finished reading the letter, Charles took it from me.

He finished it and said, "This is nobody but Joshua's buffoonery."

"I don't guess he knows that you are not alone. Does he actually think I'm nothing? This is beginning to irritate me, how misinformed he is."

Several days ago, it reached Charles that Joshua was planning to kill him. What scared me most was the fact that Charles had no fear. He may have shown himself as being worried or concerned, but it was only out of the best interest of me. He was so sure that his plan would work that he didn't care about himself. His plan didn't consist of me, but I was determined to enter into an agreement of helping, even though Charles didn't want me to become involved. He kept me in his presence, but to him, that was enough. Little did he know, when he left me at my mom's hotel room, I would sneak out and go to a gun range with Chico to learn how to shoot a gun. I wanted to be prepared for the worst. And from the plan that was given…I knew I had to. One day I almost became a suspect in a lineup by Charles. Charles had come to pick me up early and my mother told him I went to the store. He was so afraid that something was going to happen to me. He began to become a little paranoid. I had to sit him down and have a conversation with him on the subject. Ever since the conversation, he has eased up and left me to make my decisions on where I wanted to go. He didn't think he was doing anything wrong but only felt he was protecting me. He soon realized how vexing he was becoming. I always wanted to be the best at seeing that he was happy so, I kept my traveling at a minimum.

Even though it was only a week later, it felt like months. Time was slipping by and I had no way to stop it. I gained some respect from Chico, who had helped me learn to shoot. He had become an interesting person to know. He was not a father and he had never fallen in love.

I asked him one day, "So, you never want to be in love Chico?"

"Yeah, I do. But she will have to accept me da' way I am and nothing less."

Turns out, he was an a-heck-of-a instructor. He guided me in a way that left me relaxed with I pulled the trigger. In some twisted kind of way, I found myself thrilled at pulling that trigger. I didn't want Charles to find out so, I begged for Chico not to tell him. He agreed only if I would help him out in some other way. He wanted me to hook him up with someone I knew.

"I want her to look sumptin' like you Samone. I tink' you are fine." He never came on to me and I was so glad about that.

"Alright, I know someone who's really pretty. Her name is Janice Carlbright."

"Where have I heard of dat' name befor," Chico thought out loud.

"Maybe you have seen her around," I laughed.

"Wat' you laufin' for?"

"Oh, no reason," I interjected, "if you say so."

"I think you two would fit great together." I was being very dishonest, for I knew Janice would kill me if she knew what I was doing.

"Well anyway, hook me up den'."

"Alright, I will. Give me some time to set it up, though."

Not knowing my true intentions, Chico went along with the joke. The truth of the matter was, I didn't know of too many girls that would like Chico. The only person that came to mind was Janice. I wasn't going to allow the two of them to meet; I was just trying to buy myself some time. I wanted to give Chico what he wanted because of what he was doing for me. He was a nice guy, just mixed up with the wrong things. I didn't realize the upper hand he gave me in the situation. Whether he wanted to or not, he gave me power. Not the average kind of person would want this sort of power but of one who was mad. And I was the latter. I wanted revenge on what they did to me and my mother. Revenge was going to happen.

I wanted to try and get to know more about Charles. Apparently, he had a history that I wasn't clear about. So, I took advantage of the time Chico and I spent together at the gun range.

"Chico," I called out. He answered me with a movement of his head.

"I want to know what Charles did for you."

"Look, Samone I want you to kno' sumptin'. What CB did for me was the greatest and mos' respectful thing anyone has eva' done for me."

"So, are you going to share what it was?"

"I don't know if I want you to kno' just yet. I mean, CB might git' mad at me fo' tellin' you." The more I pushed him to tell me the angrier he became.

"No, Samone! I ain't tellin' you nothin' till CB tell me too. He has my loyalty." I sighed with disappointment and ached with anger.

I had to find out what happened. Charles had gained so much respect from a group of Latinos it made me wonder what they would not do for him. If Chico wasn't going to tell me, I was going to find out a different way. Maybe one of Chico's girls knew what happened; I thought to myself one day. He must have told them. Chico told me a lot about how he didn't have anyone he could trust. The only person that held that kind of trust was, of course, Charles.

"He gave me my ego back, Samone. I was just so distraught after Luis died. I had no guidance; I was only 18. Luis taught me everything I knew about loyalty and trust. And there were only a few people he trusted." I felt somewhat bad for him.

Some sympathy was displayed with what I told him, "Well, now you have someone else you can trust."

He smiled and said, "Oh, do I really?"

"Yes, you do. Chico." We embraced each other for a split second and turned our attention back to business.

"I tink' you got it, Samone. You don't need me no mo'. But I will help you with anything else you need. Okay?"

"Thanks, and I will keep that in mind." That was the last time I saw Chico.

CHAPTER THREE

"Samone come here. I want to tell you what I did for the Latinos," Charles commanded the next day.

We were out in the park walking when I turned around to find Charles sitting down on a bench. Inside I was ecstatic. I've been longing to know what happened ever since we entered that house. I walked over to the bench and sat down.

"Well, it all started about two years ago," he paused before he finished, "I gave Luis a proper burial and I help save Chico's life. He needed someone to guide him back into the life of the living. Chico didn't care about life at the time and he almost still doesn't care." Charles warned.

"That's it? That's the big secret?"

"Well, I'm not finished. I also found him a heart donor. Chico had a bad heart and he was going to die. Since I work at the hospital, I was able to match his heart with someone who passed away. Don't ask me how I did it, but know that it took a lot of work to find him one and I succeeded. That's why he is in debt with me."

"Oh wow, Charles. That is a great thing you did. I see why he owes you so much. But what I don't understand is why the secret? Why did it take you so long to tell me something like that? Did you know him at the time?"

"No, I didn't know him personally. I knew of him by some newspapers. Stories were done about a young Latino male needing a heart," Charles began to look out unto the pond. I studied his face and realized that there was more to the story.

"I'm also his brother."

"What? How is that possible?"

"My mother and his father are now married."

My mouth popped opened and I closed it right after a fly tried to guide itself in it. I had to admit this was a story to have waited upon telling.

"I'm used to it just being my sister and I, but that was supposed to be it. Chico doesn't have siblings and his mother died when he was six."

"So, that's why you took your time in telling me."

"Yes, I thought you wouldn't accept me on the account of him. Samone, he is bad news," Charles pleaded with his eyes, "I want you not to trust him. He may seem like he will do no wrong, but I've witnessed him doing things unheard of."

"Charles, I believe he trusts and admires you for what you did for him. I think he would do anything for you."

"Yes, I know. But that doesn't mean he's not dangerous. I have his loyalty, but that's it." He grabbed my hand and kissed it.

"I don't want anything to happen to you."

"Nothing will as long as I have God and you." He smiled. We stood up and preceded on to finish our walk.

"I have a strong feeling that everything is going to be alright."

"I do too, Charles. I do too."

"Chico, what's up Man? Are you ready for tonight?"

"Yeah, Man. I'm ready. And so is the crew."

I looked at Chico with a different light and I could tell he was different than what Charles had said. His charisma told me a lot. He wanted more than what was offered to him. He desired something different, something that included change.

"Good. Now, this is what you guys need to do. Stay within 50 feet of each other and watch each other's back when we make it there. I know the whole layout of Joshua's pad, but I don't know how many guards he may have."

Charles laid a blueprint of Joshua's home on the table. Who was this man, I wondered? I was amazed at how he was able to gain knowledge of things. He knew me like an open book and now he was displaying to me that he knew more about Joshua than I ever will. He had access to things I didn't believe anyone could get their hands on. I grew numb to what I was feeling about Joshua; I knew he was in deep trouble. A hit was made out for his life and I knew about it. I knew all the details and the way that they were going to do it. Charles took his time and explained every object on the blueprint. It was a great estate. A place I had never been. In the two years I've known Joshua, he never revealed to me this particular place. The only discovery I was permitted to learn was that of his condo. Joshua's estate was far beyond my imagination. I thought about the time Michelle said to me, *"Maybe it's just a test...."* It had to be. Joshua didn't need me. He wanted me. I looked over at Charles, who was planning a detailed entry to Joshua's estate to win his property. I couldn't imagine the things that Charles would do if he knew that I felt somewhat distraught over the whole ordeal. He would probably pitch a fit and exclaim that I was still romantically in love with him. I didn't care for Joshua anymore. He was out of my system.

"Samone, are you going to be ok with knowing you could have stopped this," something whispered in my ear? I ignored the voice, for I knew it was my mind playing tricks on me.

"Are you sure dis' will work?" Chico asked.

My mind began to flow in and out of the conversation that was going on between Chico and his crew and Charles. I wanted to know what was going on, but I couldn't concentrate.

"Are you going to be ok with knowing you could have stopped this," the voice repeated itself.

"Stop it!" Everybody looked from the blueprint to face me with alarm.

"Stop what, Samone?" questioned everybody.

"What's going on with you?" Charles asked while taking my hand.

"Are you ok?" Chico said.

Feeling mortified, I try to say with the steadiest voice, "I'm fine."

"Are you sure? Because if you can't handle this, you may need to step out," Charles said in a stern tone.

"Yeah, I'm sure. I just had a moment." With that, everyone went back to studying the blueprint.

Was I losing my mind? Was it intended of me to stop this plan? I didn't know what it was that came over me, but I felt like I was being watched. I felt that my actions were being written down and defined in a book of record. I had to stop and sit down to try to recuperate from the overwhelming feeling of panic. Charles glanced my way but kept with his plan of action.

"This will all go down at seven p.m. tonight, so I need everyone in position."

Charles knew how to take charge in a situation, which was different to me. I was used to a bashful man who took orders and did not give them. At least that was what I thought. Apparently, I was gravely mistaken.

Resisting what had taken place, I said, "Charles, let me do something. I want to help."

"Samone sit down. This is not the time or place. I already told you, I don't want you to be involved."

"But I am involved," I insisted.

"I don't kno' homs'...maybe she can distract Joshua somehow." Charles pondered on the thought for a minute and decided against it.

"She kno' him. What do you tink'?"

"Chico, my fiancé, is very naive when it comes to this type of business. She would be better off if she didn't get involved."

That was it. No one else mentioned anything about me being a part of the biggest heist that was about to go down in reference to a drug lord. After I sat there, I began to become irritated. I needed some air. I left them, all of them that were there reading the blueprint and exchanging vocabulary. Here I was, a perfect way to get Joshua's attention and no one took me seriously, well…except Chico. He knew what I was capable of when it came to shooting a gun. Too bad he didn't have the power to convince Charles that I could be a useful pawn in his plan. It wasn't quite time for them to go, but I wanted to prove to Charles that I could be as creative as he was. It was now or never that I should go to the estate of Joshua.

It was 6:30 when I arrived at the estate, Camp Rambo, as the blueprint called it. I was all alone but didn't have a fear or worry in my bones. I was about to prove that I could do some damage as well. I decided that I wasn't the goody-too-shoe that everyone thought I was. I knew better than to just walk in Joshua's pad with nothing to protect me, so I popped Charles's trunk hoping to find something useful that would help me. I inspected the trunk and low and behold, a couple of guns were there waiting for me. I grabbed one and checked it for bullets. It was loaded. I strapped the gun to my ankle and walked to the front of the castle-like gates. I was soon approached by one of the guards.

"Who are you? And what do you want?"

"I'm Samone Gray and I'm here to see.."

Before I could finish my thought, he interjected with, "Are you really Samone Gray?"

"Yes, I am. And if it's not too much trouble, I would like to chat with Mr. Franks." The guard gave me an incurable grimace and opened the gate.

"Be safe now and have a great day," he said sarcastically. I walked through the gate with my head to the sky.

"Lord, take care of me and forgive me for what I'm about to do," I silently said.

Once I finished the hike up the marble hill, I saw his mansion with my own eyes. I marveled at what I had seen. It was covered with windows to let in the light from the day. The entrance door stood about 24 feet high and 36 inches wide. The doors were made up of maple wood and were embedded in a structure that stood upon concrete ground. The building consisted of red and white bricks, installed lights, and security cameras. I wanted to see what was inside. I knew that it had to be just as beautiful. Just when I was about to ring the doorbell, Joshua opened the door. His boyish smile startled me. I wasn't expecting him to be delightful to me.

"Samone, do come in."

He stepped aside and allowed me to enter. He wasn't alone. Joshua had company and they were with him in the foyer.

"Joshua, who is this?" the woman asked.

"This is Samone. The woman I told you about."

"Oh, her." The woman got up from the chair and picked up the small child from the floor.

"So, how did you learn of my place?"

I looked at him, I then reached for him to hug me, but he refused to do so. I didn't know why I acted upon such impulse, but I was hoping that I could clear the air. I stared after the walking mother and the baby in the arms. From the glimpse of the small child, he looked like him. He had the same nose and eyes. He was a handsome baby. I would have been proud to be the stepmother to him.

"Samone, are you going to answer me?"

"I found out through a friend of mine," I said, turning to face him.

"Some friends you have. No one really knows about this place. The only people who do have either been here or I have told them about it. I wasn't expecting you to be so kind to give yourself up. Especially since you have a different love." He led me to a table that was by the kitchen.

"Sit down, I want to talk."

"I see that you have company; I don't want to keep you," I suggested. I turned to go, but he blocked my path to the door.

"No, Samone. You are not going anywhere. I don't know who you think you are to come to my place and show yourself then think that you can leave as you please. Woman, I loved you," he growled.

He walked up on me and I took a step back. He kept coming and I took more backward steps till I didn't have anywhere to go. He pinned me to the wall and slapped me.

"Stop Joshua!" I yelled.

He kept hitting me and the more he did the more I screamed, but to his satisfaction, no one came to my rescue. At first, when I saw the child, I thought about telling him what Charles was up to. But I changed my mind. I shielded my face and slid to the floor. He stood towering over me. He spat upon me like I was the ground outside. That's when I grabbed the gun from my ankle. It was in his sight to see, so he froze in one spot.

I said through my sobs, "Stop! You will not lay your hand on me again."

"How could you bring that gun in my home, Samone?" he asked.

"The same way you thought it was okay to beat me."

This time it was I who cornered him. While pointing the gun at him, the woman entered the room.

She screamed, "Samone, please put the gun down. I won't hit you anymore!" From the corner of my eye, I saw the woman easing toward my way.

"I think you better stop right there. As a matter of fact, since you want to come in here and be nosy, get over there by him." She walked to where Joshua was standing.

"Why? Samone, why?" he pleaded.

"The same reason you captured my mother and trashed my apartment. Remember that?"

"Look, Samone. That's just stuff. I can't take back what I did, but I can make it up to you. I have a son now."

"Shut up Joshua! I don't want to hear nothing else from you."

By this time, it was 7 o'clock. It was my intention to do something, but now it was all a mess.

"Joshua, what is the real reason you captured my mother?"

"I took her because Michelle convinced me to. She told me about

Charles and I was so hurt. I couldn't bare the pain alone, so I wanted you to hurt too."

"You are so evil Joshua. Everyone thinks that I'm a saint; well, I'm going to prove everyone wrong."

At that moment, I heard gunshots. Joshua and the woman looked at each other with fear in their eyes.

"What's going on Samone?"

"You know what? I really came over here to tell you so that we could clear the air. But you had to lay your hands on me and spit on me like I'm some kind of dog. How could you do that to me?" Charles entered the room to find me holding the two of them hostage.

"Samone, what are you doing? This is not your fight."

"Charles, stop treating me like I'm some kind of angel...." Charles looked me over with horror in his eyes, "...which one should I shoot first?"

"No one Samone. You know this was not the plan."

"Forget the plan. I want him to suffer." Evidently, the guns woke up the baby and he started screaming at the top of his lungs.

"What is that?" Charles looked around to answer his own question but found none.

"Oh, that's Joshua's soon-to-be bastard son."

"Samone, what is wrong with you?" Charles walked over to my side and reached for the gun, but I moved it from his reach.

"Samone, please hand over the gun...." Charles then turned his attention to the woman, "...go and get the baby." The woman walked swiftly to the other room to console the child.

"Charles, I don't trust her. She might try and do something. Go and get her."

Charles didn't take my command lightly; he understood what I was getting at. He decided to go retrieve the woman and child.

"Hey Samone, what are you getting from all of this?"

"…an overwhelming feeling of comfort. I was so close to tell you what will happen to you."

"You still can," he whimpered.

"No, I can't. You messed everything up."

"No, Samone. You messed everything up," Charles said while entering the room with the woman and child.

He looked to be angry and that disturbed my mood. I didn't want him to be angry with me. I loved him so dearly. Yet and still, I manage to do the very thing I dreaded to do.

"Were you going to tell him our secrets?" he asked.

"No, I was going to try and clear the air for all of us. He spat on me and beat me with his knuckles."

"I see that. That's why I didn't want you to be involved. If you would have stayed away, this would have never happened."

There was silence in the room; even the crying Jamal seemed interested in hearing what I was going to say. Charles walked to my side and placed his hand upon my shoulder.

"Samone. You can't do this. This is not your battle but mine. You will be my wife soon and there is nothing that you can do to please me more than you to just let me handle the battle." Charles eased his hand over the gun and took it from me. I sobbed and wanted to feel protected again.

He put me in his arms and told me, "Here is your ring; put it back on."

I hesitated for a moment and then slid the ring on. Joshua glared at me. He didn't even seem to notice Charles there saying soothing words to me to save his life.

"Thank you for the help, Charles. Now can you and your mad fiancé get out of my house?"

"Oh no, Joshua. There is still much work to be done," Charles declined.

Joshua then put up his hands and said, "I give up. Take whatever it is you want, but spare my life for the sake of my son."

"Do you really think I care about your child?"

Joshua started to beg for his life. And honestly, it was humiliating. I wish I would have shot that gun. No man deserves to be alive after what he did to me.

"Samone, go to the car and drive home."

"Hey homs', all the guards are dead," Chico interjected. He walked into the room with an AK-47 in his hand while looking perplexed at what he had seen.

"Wat's goin' on here," he asked.

"I thought I killed you. You and that good for nothing Luis," Joshua boasted. Chico looked at him with murderous eyes.

"I tink' I want to take 'em right here and now, CB."

"Nah, not right now. I told you what I want to do with him."

"Yeah, but he is disgracing mi' hombre Luis. Lemme' do it."

"Charles, let me do it," I added.

Charles was confused from the pleading and he tampered out the words, "Hell to the no to the both of you. I said we were going to take him back to headquarters." Both Chico and I stood silent.

"So, I see you are more prepared than I thought, Charles. But you forgot that I have people that I know as well. And this gang of people you have here now will never be enough. Take me where you will, but my people will be after you soon enough."

"Joshua. Just know my plan is in the beginning stages. Your people will be carefully taken care of."

I had no idea what Charles was speaking of. He was talking like a mastermind. He gave out instructions to Chico and me. Chico left the room with his tongue-speaking Spanish. On the other hand, I did as I was told, but I lingered around as long as I could. When I left Charles, he had Joshua tied up and his mouth covered so he couldn't hear the threats anymore.

I couldn't blame Charles for shutting up all the trash talking and swearing coming from Joshua's mouth. Out of the house, I went. While I was on my way to Charles's car, I noticed a figure lingering around the car.

I asked, "Who is there?" I received no answer, but the figure stood there facing me. It was Chico.

"Chico, what are you trying to do? Scare the Jesus out of me?"

"Aw Samone, com' on now. I wouldn't want to do dat'. Do you believe Charles is going to stick to the plan," he asked, cutting right to the chase.

"Knowing Charles, he probably is. I know he seem to be out of his mind right now with all of the plans he is making, but he will do what is planned."

"I'm sure he will. Dats' not what I'm getting at." I walked closer to him to see him vexed and uncontrollably shaking.

"What's wrong with you? Why are you shaking?"

"Wat' do anybody care?"

"Chico, I care." I reached to grab him and he allowed me to hug him.

When I released him, there was blood on my hands.

"What happened to you?"

"I got stabbed a while ago. It's okay; I will be fine."

"No, Chico. Let me take you to the hospital."

"I would, but I alrady' have mi' Amiga taking me. If you need anything, let me know, Samone."

"Are you sure you don't need my assistance? I mean, where is your hombre at? I don't see anybody."

"Here I am," I heard a small voice coming from the bushes say; it was a female.

She looked to be in her 20s. She had a small body but seemed to carry a huge load of attitude. She brushed past me. I was then able to see her face in the dim light of the night. She wore an eye patch, which ironically had a peace sign on it. She had full lips and she looked to be a Black female.

"I got it from here Samone." With that, she allowed Chico to lean on her shoulders while they walked away.

I didn't mean to stare, but I couldn't help it. She looked so out of place trying to help a 6'5 man.

"Samone. What are you doing? I thought I told you to leave." I turned to face Charles.

"I was, but I was just stopped by Chico. He was stabbed."

"What!?! Where is he?"

"He is gone with the girl with the patch."

"Oh, that's Lena. He will be fine with her. She got mad skills in surviving." I opened the car door, but Charles turned me to face him. He kissed me and he told me that the job was done.

"What do you mean? I thought you were going to take him to headquarters."

"Change of plans. He kept pleading... Well, you will never have to hear from him again. He's gone."

"He's gone?"

"Yes."

I was hit with a horrible anguished sensation that overpowered me. I didn't realize that he was going to kill him. I thought I would be able to handle it. I bent over to take in a couple of breaths.

"You still love him, don't you?" Charles inquired. There was silence.

"No, Charles. It is you that I love. I am your rib," I said, standing up to face him.

That made him so happy to hear. He picked me up in a hug and kiss.

"With all the things that have happened here tonight, I'm glad that I still have you."

"Charles, let's get out of here." We both got in the car and Charles drove away.

And as we were leaving, I saw figures in the night running in and out of Joshua's mansion. I soon saw fire coming from his mansion. It was over the battle had been won by Charles. I would never see that handsome face of Joshua's again. I would never hear his breath panting lightly as we rested through the night. It was over. It was the end of a chapter in my book. A part of my life that would never be read again. It was dark, but the sky was red with fire and the smoke filled the air.

"Charles, what did you do with the woman and child?"

"Don't worry Samone. They were let free."

I felt an emptiness in my stomach. I was longing to hold the old Joshua that I once knew. He was now gone. We sat through the duration of our trip in silence.

We were home with mixed emotions about the events that took place. Charles sat on the couch to relax. I sat down across from him. The air was rich with despair and we seemed to lose touch with reality.

"Charles. What happened when I left?"

"Samone, I really prefer that you do not know. It's not right in what happened and I will have to live with it for the rest of my life."

I started to feel the pain that he felt. He seemed different. It was a kind of different that showed when someone took a life.

"Are you okay, Charles?" He didn't say anything but just looked out in the dimmed room.

"I almost got killed tonight," he murmured. I didn't say anything, only waited for him to finish his thoughts. "...I didn't think I cared that much about life until it was almost taken away from me. It's powerful, you know, the creation of man. I only kept thinking about you when I was seeing that Joshua was taken care of. I wanted to know some information from him before the job was finished. So, I removed the tape from his lips. He managed to slip in the words, "Take care of her. Samone. And make sure that my son is taken care of."" Charles began to whimper and then it turned into sobs of tears. He showed no emotion through his tears.

"Charles, you got to believe that what was done was done for good reason. Joshua wasn't going to stop until my family or I was dead. You must believe that."

"Look, I'm going to take a shower. Would you do me the favor of checking on Chico?"

Charles gave me the number to Lena and he exited the living room. I looked at him while he walked and his head was hanging in a remorseful way. I pitied him. Right then and there, I knew that I was going to make this up to him. He was my heart and it ached because of the pain he displayed in his words and in his face. Joshua was the killer that I knew. Charles was not someone who desired to kill but rather punish. It was a big difference between the two.

I dialed the number given to me and on the first ring, Lena answered the phone, "CB is that you? Chico is in the hospital in critical condition."

My eyes widen with fear of the death of Chico, "No, Lena it's Samone. Charles asked that I call you to find out how he was doing?"

"Oh, he's not doing so well. He lost a lot of blood. Are y'all coming to see him?"

"Of course! As soon as possible."

"Okay, I will tell him. Hurry."

"We will."

"Charles," he is in critical condition, I said while entering the bathroom.

"Really? We must go then." Charles was out of the shower and instantly dressed before I took my medicine.

"Good, you remembered to take that."

"Yeah, it is. Let's go now."

I could see the weariness in his eyes. He was tired and so was I. Our bodies were being powered off by the second burst of energy that we didn't know we had. I wanted to desperately rid myself of the filth of the night. But Chico was more important. Inside the car, a sense of disturbance happened. Charles was blaming himself for Chico's stabbing and driving like a maniac. He was going to need help himself that night. I tried to calm him down with words that were given to me within my spirit.

"Listen to me Charles. The Bible says this, *'And we know that all things work together for good to them that love God, to them who are the called according to His purpose.'* Let's reason with this."

I don't know what those words meant, but it worked. He completely let me know that he believed in those words by slowing the speed of the car.

"Is it really," he asked.

"Samone, what we did tonight is not good. Does that scripture apply to us?"

"Yes, it does. We love God. And we are within his purpose."

I didn't know if Charles was a spiritual man, but he proved that he was when he asked, "Why does God allow us to hurt one another and have no fear of what he will do to us because of it?"

"God is love Charles. And yet we are his to give eternal life to…we still have to make the decision to do his will. It is the God in us that keeps us in his purpose. So, when the next time something like this happens, we have to make a better decision."

"Okay. I will have to do better."

"We both will," I agreed.

When we made it to the hospital, there was chaos. No one wanted to wait on us. It took about 30 minutes before a nurse asked us who we wanted to visit.

"Chico Hernandez, please." Charles stated to the nurse that it was a matter of urgency.

"I do understand your request Sir, but unfortunately, he has been moved to ICU. No one has been given permission to see him."

We couldn't believe our ears. We sat down with no air in our lungs. Our hopes of seeing our friend had been depleted with no sympathy of any kind.

"Hey. CB come here!" a familiar voice yelled. Both of our eyes looked to see Lena standing in the hallway.

"He's asking to see you!" Charles rushed to Lena; it was as if he flew.

I stood outside the room with Lena, who was in her own world. She decided to let me in her world, for she asked me

"What took you guys so long? He is about to die, isn't he?" she asked.

"I don't know Lena. Hopefully, he won't."

Joy had been taken from her soul; I felt it. She stood there with distance between her and me. She beckoned for me to come here.

"I want you to know that he only wanted to win CB's love. No one really cares for him because of his past. The only person who showed they had any respect is Charles." Charles came out of the room with tears in his eyes.

"My friend is going to die."

"Lena, you mustn't say anything like that. He will live. I know it," Charles let out a cry of pain… "it's my entire fault."

I tried to do my best to better their spirits, but it was too much for me to bear. Even I had my own moan of sorrow to reason with. The young surgeon, Dr. Stewart, who had stitched me up, came to our aid to supply us with information regarding the latest news on Chico.

"Well, I'm sorry to say that your friend has been given morphine to subdue the pain. He is not coherent right now. He will be sedated if need be. His condition has worsened over the hours, but we have stopped the bleeding. The best thing for you all to do is go home."

"Dr. Stewart, will he live?"

"It's hard to say, Ms. Gray. We can only wait it out at this point."

"Will you let us know if anything changes?"

"Yes Sir, I will."

"Thank you," Lena said. She stuck out her hand and he shook it.

"You guys, be safe going home. I hear there's a major fire that has spread throughout the southern part of the city."

"Thanks, Dr. Stewart, we will."

CHAPTER FOUR

He was breathing hard throughout that whole night. He was sound to sleep when I heard a voice speak to me... *"You had the chance to clear the air. Look what you have done...."* I shook my head violently and woke Charles up.

"Baby, are you okay?"

"Oh Charles, I can't take this. This is too much for me to handle."

"What are you talking about?" I didn't want him to know of the voices I had been hearing, so I improvised with a reason.

"Charles, I don't know. Maybe it's all the things that have been happening...Chico, Joshua, and the fire. I just need to be left alone."

"Alright, if that's what you want."

Charles was about to go to the couch when I said, "Charles, it was a mistake to tell you that. Please get back into bed."

"Samone."

"Don't worry. It won't happen again." He climbed back into bed where his back was to me.

I didn't argue, for I knew he had much on his mind. While the love of my life drifted back to sleep, I laid there so desperately wanting to do the same. Looking to the left of me, I witnessed the rain that had begun to pour. He was doing me a favor, helping me to be able to rest as Charles did. I knew deep down that God cared for me. Even though I had a funny way of showing it, I loved Him too.

So, I prayed that night and to my surprise, He answered me with sweet words, "I love you. Be blessed in the things that you do, for I am with you." I tugged at the covers that Charles had snatched and I dozed off as well.

Dr. Stewart called Charles and announced that Chico was doing better. I thought that it would be nice for Chico to see Charles, even though Charles did not want to go. Charles thought that his close call to death had been his fault. He didn't want to face the man that stood in the line of fire for his cause. I persuaded Charles to go and visit his brother, who desperately needed to see a comforting face. Chico admired him and Charles was so oblivious to the fact that it blinded him.

"Charles, Chico needs you right now. Won't you pay him respect?" As I convinced him, he sat in silence, listening to everything I had to say.

"You are right, Baby. I will be with him in his time of need. Thanks for reminding me of how Chico views me." With that, we headed to the hospital to find him sitting upright in his bed, smiling at Lena.

"Hey, my main man. I'm glad to see you doing better."

"CB wats' up. Come and sit, tell me whats ben' goin' on."

"Hey, Chico. I see you are doing good," I said, sitting beside Charles.

"Oh hey, Samone. Yeah, I'm doin' good. I could be betta' if dey' let me out of here."

"We were just talking about you two. How we wanted to attend the grand wedding of the century," Lena announced. Everyone let out a laugh.

"Good morning, everyone. It's good to see everyone in a good mood." Everyone turned their eyes to meet one of the nurses as she entered the door.

"Hello," everyone said. The nurse took it and smiled, then returned to us an official greeting.

"The doctor should be here in a minute. He wanted to fill you all in on the results of Chico's MRI."

"Thank you nurse," Charles acknowledged. The nurse made sure every machine was accurate.

"Hmmph." The nurse looked at his heart monitor.

"Wat's wrong, nurse?"

"Mr. Hernandez, you do have a donor heart, right?" The mood of the room changed from gladness to a very stern one.

"Yeah, why?"

"Well, it looks to me that your heart rate is stronger than we anticipated."

"That's a good thing, right?" Lena asked without hesitation.

"Well, of course, Ms. Bradley. I will let the doctor answer any other questions or concerns; until then, is there anything else that you need while I'm here?" I considered the thing; Chico loved all the attention that he was getting.

"Nah, nurse, I have everything I need right here."

"Alright. Let us know if that changes." The nurse took her tray with empty medicine and walked out.

"Wow, Chico. You have a heart of gold."

"You know what, Charles you are right," Lena and I agreed.

"Aww. You don't have to say such words to me CB. I aldedy' know."

Chico beamed with delight. He took it in stride by accepting the notion of Charles to uplift his spirits. Dr. Stewart walked into the room while clearing his throat.

"Uhmm mm. Good morning, everyone."

Everyone faced the doctor with appreciated facial expressions, "Good morning."

"As you may know, Chico was struck close to a nerve in his back. It was inches from causing horrific maneuverable problems. It's a miracle that he can still move. I know that you are itching to know when you can go home, Chico, but we still need to run more tests on you. We want to make sure that it is safe for you to be at home as an outpatient. So, with that being said, you may go home in a couple of weeks. Get well soon and keep your movement to a minimum. We don't want you to tear those stitches."

"Thanks, Dr. Stewart. And I won't tear my stitches."

"Good to see friendly faces in here for moral support. If you all have any further questions, please feel free to contact me personally. I'm here to help."

The Dr. left us staring at one another with silent questions of what will happen next. Charles wanted to share his plan with the one man that could pull it off, but he was limited to what he could say in public. The last plan did not go as planned because of me. I didn't want to be the blame for the failures of the next plan. I had learned my lesson and I wanted to help in other ways. The big drop was going to happen in a few days; accordingly, to Michelle and Tyrone, they wanted the money from Joshua. Only Joshua was no more. They would have to come to me to get it. It was their last option and Charles was preparing himself for the last two people on the list. He had come up with a plan that was sure to work but only if I could carry out the orders perfectly. I really admired all the thought and effort Charles' put in his pursuit of capturing the last two criminals. This time I was going to let the two bad guys suffer the consequences for their actions behind bars. That was the initial plan for Joshua. I figured that Charles had to do what he did because a gun was presented on the scene. Everyone knows that you don't threaten someone's life with a gun with no intentions of using it. It would literally be a dead cause. I didn't believe Charles to be a man that would take a life. He never admitted to it; he just said that he was gone. To cater the thought of innocence being a part of our relationship, I convinced myself that he didn't pull the trigger.

"Samone, are you okay? You seem distracted," Lena uttered.

"I'm okay, just thinking about things."

"Yeah, I kno' da' feelin'. I've ben' doin' a lot of that myself. I can't get into detail bout' what I tink' about."

We all understood exactly what he meant. No hidden secrets would be exposed in the hospital today.

"You know, I have a secret to tell you all. I've been waiting for the right time to dispose of this but have never had the chance." Charles had everyone's attention. When there was no response, Charles proceeded with telling his secret.

"It's a matter of time before the war will begin and I've prepared myself. I'm not so sure what to do after everything is done. But my secret is, I have no blood on my hands. I have never killed anyone. What was done to Joshua was never my intention, but what is done is done. I know this is not the time or place to discuss such madness; I just had to relieve myself of the pain. Samone, just know that whatever happens in the next few days, I love you."

Chico and Lena were just as surprised as I was to hear such words of choice that had departed from Charles' mouth. We didn't know what to say, so we just sat and stared at him with the bleakest expression.

"Why are y'all looking at me like that?"

"Lik' what homs'?"

"Like, y'all don't have any concern about what I said."

"We do have concern about what you said. Maybe I have too much concern. Look around, Charles. Look where you are at. There is no real privacy here."

I paid no attention to what Lena had said and voiced my opinion, "Maybe we should just let Captain Haynes handle this."

"Wait, wait, wait… Samone, you outta' order for bringin' dat hombre name up."

"Let's all just cool out and just wait till we have some privacy," Lena butted in.

It was agreed that we should wait. Charles looked at me with pleading eyes. I didn't know what it meant. What was he thinking of doing? The words "whatever happens" just kept replaying in my thoughts. I wanted to know what this man was up to.

"Samone, would you please answer your phone?" I looked at Lena and then pulled out my phone.

"Hello."

"Yes, may I speak with Ms. Gray, please?"

"This is she. Who is this?"

"This is Captain Haynes with the Austin Police Department. May I have a moment of your time? Some things have come up and your name is all in the mix." I gasped for air and tried to get my heart to pumping again.

"Okay, Captain Haynes. Sure I will meet you at the station in an hour." I hung up the phone and saw the bewildered faces looking at me.

"Wat' is dat' all about?"

"The Captain said that some things have come up and that my name is all in the mix," I muttered, "I wonder what it could be, Samone."

I looked at Charles then replied, "I don't know, but I have to meet him in an hour."

"Yeah, I know. Well, Chico, I think the Captain just crashed the party. We will be back later."

"A'ight homs' y'all take care and let me kno' what happens."

"Sure Chico. See you later, Lena."

"Bye. Samone, remember that your silence is expected."

For some reason, I just wanted to punch her in the face. Of course, I knew that silence was the key. I knew not to open my mouth.

"Sure, Lena, I'll try to remember that," I hissed with sarcasm.

She gave me a dirty look to let me know that she was well aware of my sarcasm. To avoid a physical fight between the two of us, Charles stepped in between us.

"Alright ladies, let's try and be civil here."

"There's nothing going on here. Right, Samone?"

"Right." Charles knew that it was a bit of hostility seeping between Lena and myself.

"I don't know what has gotten into the two of you, but just stop it. We need to be on the same team here. So, just squash this." Neither one of us said a word.

"Is it squashed?"

"Well, I was only reminding Samone to just keep her mouth shut."

"And I was only agreeing. Although, I feel that she didn't need to make that known to me. I mean, why would I jeopardize our situation? Heck, I'm involved in this too." Lena realized her mistake in mentioning my mouth to be closed. She apologized and I accepted.

"A'ight then, good this is squashed." Charles guided my waist out of the door.

Once we entered the hallway, he whispered in my ear, "I liked your feistiness. I thought it was about to be a cat fight." I smiled with disbelief.

He winked his eye at me and returned the smile. This man was proving to be totally different than what I imagined. Who was this Charles Lucas Brown?

We arrived at the police station and waited for the Captain to appear in his brown suit and tie.

"Thanks for coming down so fast. It's urgent that I speak with you."

"What is this about Captain Haynes," I asked worriedly.

"Well, you should follow me to my office so there will be more privacy."

He led the way; as we were following, I asked Charles, "Could I be in trouble?"

Charles assured me that I wasn't the one in trouble and that I shouldn't worry. For some reason, I believed different. It was the way the Captain was acting. He was performing as if he had solved a case and was ready to put the suspect behind bars. We entered the room, which seemed to be somewhat organized. Charles and I actually had somewhere to sit.

"Okay, I'm going to break right to the point, Samone. I received an anonymous call the other day. And the caller said that they saw you at the house of Joshua Franks on the night of the fire. Is this true?" I looked at Charles as if he had been asked the question.

"No, I wasn't there. Who is the caller that told you that?"

"Well, Ms. Gray. The caller said you were there. I usually don't inquire off of he say she say nonsense, but the caller was very convincing. So, you do need to tell me the truth. Tell me if you were there."

"I wasn't there, Captain. Honestly, why would I be seen at Joshua Frank's house when I know nothing about it?"

The Captain looked me over to spy out any mysteries that should be known. He was in deep consideration that I could have been telling the truth.

"Samone, I have no objection in believing your answer, but I will continue this investigation and for your sake, I do hope you are telling the truth."

His voice was so cold that it sent a chilling sensation through the core of my truth. I wanted so badly to tell my truth, but it was then put on ice. I needed to wait till the right time to speak the truth. Captain Haynes' eyes began to search for the truth. They went from me then across to Charles. There was silence in the room. It was as if the Captain was waiting for us to break his interrogation. His path was pointing toward the truth and I had decided to take the opposite direction.

"I don't know if I can just shake off what I've been told. I don't know what I can do for you, so in the meantime, I will need for you to stay in the city limits of Austin."

"Captain! Are you blaming me for the fire? What is it that is going on? It can't be for the simple fact of he say she say garbage. This is my life here."

"She is right, Captain. You are going to the extreme of things for a simple word on the street. What's really going on?"

"I'll tell you what's going on. Once all the evidence is presented in my hands, I will know from experience the truth. So, go on and leave. I will let you know what the outcome reveals. Don't leave the city, for if you do…you will be placed in jail."

"Captain, surely you can't believe this so-called caller over me. You have the recordings of crazy people looking for me. Isn't that enough? You also haven't told me if you believe I started the fire."

"Look, I'm done. I don't have to take orders, I don't have to answer questions, neither do I usually inquire questions from potential suspects. But when I feel I've been lied to... it makes me upset. So, go ahead and leave... while you still can."

We could see that there was no gaining further information from the Captain, also no changing his mind. By the lines on his forehead, I could tell he was surely upset. Charles and I stood to leave; as we left, I heard a phone ring.

"This is Captain Haynes..." He shooed us off with a wave of his hand as we exited the door.

He didn't hear me when I said, "Hmmph. I'm not sure if I want to know what the jail cell feels like, but I know if leaving here is my only decision, then I'm taking it." Charles didn't say anything; he left me to do all the talking. I found that was odd.

"Charles, do you hear me?"

"Yes, Samone, I do. Just got a lot on my mind, like who could be that anonymous caller?"

"I was thinking the same thing."

"I tell you what; I think it may be someone we have yet to take care of. Yeah, someone who wants you to suffer," Charles thought out loud.

I knew exactly whom Charles was speaking of. Tyrone and Michelle were the last two deviant people left on the list to take care of. The Captain was very dismissive of my approach to my defense; he was very sure of me being at Joshua's. Who could have called? No one saw me except the guards, which Chico and the crew took care of and the woman with the child. Then it hit me like a revelation from God. It must have been the woman, for she was the only person who survived the battle. I wondered what she was up to. It had to be the fact that she wanted the baby father in her life and now that he was gone, she wanted revenge. She wanted me to suffer at the hands of her. I knew that I had to make a plan of my own. If I wanted to stay alive and out of jail, I had to do a lot of praying and thinking.

"Charles, I think that the woman with the child called the Captain," I said once we were in the car.

"Yeah, I figured the same thing. She was the only person whom I allowed to be free. She was very frightened for her life. I warned her not to tell anyone about what had took place. She promised that she would not and took her baby then left. I thought that she wouldn't have the nerve to do this, but she has proved me wrong."

"Charles, the big drop is tomorrow in Dallas. How am I going to be able to go if I have to stay in Austin? You know if the last two hear of me being alone, they will come for me."

"I know they are going to come for you. Remember, you have the money. Where is the money, Samone?"

Every part of me wanted to shut up in my own shell. I wanted to disappear and go to a place that no one could find me. Everything revolved around me. Charles wanted me to be his wife; the two nutcases wanted the money of Joshua for the drop, the woman with the baby wanted revenge, Dedra was upset with me over a silly kiss… I could just go on with more things that just seemed so unreal but yet were very real.

"Charles, the money is in a separate account in a bank in Chicago."

"Chicago? Why there?" I then replied, "Because the banks there has extreme security over money in that quantity."

"It's that much, huh?"

"Yes. It wasn't supposed to be known to anyone that I had it. Joshua trusted me not to touch it for any reason at all."

"Does he have access to it?"

"The account is in my name only, but if something should happen to me he would be able to get it. He is the beneficiary on the account." I studied the question and wondered what he meant by if he had access.

"Charles, what do you mean regarding him having access to the money? Who cares if he has access to the account? He is dead."

He broke the awkward silence and said, "I think we are being followed. Don't look back." A sense of question came over me. I wasn't sure what to do and I became uneasy in my seat.

"Be still, Samone, act normal."

"Charles, how sure are you that we are being followed?"

"Oh, I'm very sure. Ever since we left the APD, I noticed him on our tail. And from looking in the review mirror, I see two figures in the car."

Great! Now we had company on the expressway where anything could happen. I sat in my seat sweating. The air in the car was not cooling me off.

"I'm going to take the next exit. I don't want this creep to know where we live."

"Charles, are you crazy? Anything can happen."

"Please, Samone, I have no choice. We have to face these clowns. Look in the glove department and give me what's inside."

I did as he commanded and found that he was speaking of a gun. He reached for. I gave it to him.

"Samone. When I pull over, stay in the car and keep your head down."

We ended up parking at a Jack in The Box restaurant. Charles turned the engine off and we sat in the car in silence. I heard the gun being cocked back to put a bullet in the chamber.

"If they want war, then that's what they will get." Charles reached for the car door to open it.

"Charles, what in the world are you doing? Stay your butt in this car. You are not invincible to bullets. Take your own advice you have given me." Charles looked at me then in the review mirror.

"Samone, get ready; here they come."

I braced myself and began to scream inside. I wanted to let go of all the fear, all the rage, all the built-up energy I had inside.

"Charles, do you have another gun?"

"No, my Love, I don't. Whatever happens, know that I tried to make it right for you and for myself. I wanted us to be together."

The two strangers were at both the driver and the passenger windows peeking in. Charles was sitting upright in his seat and I had my head down in my lap, silently praying for God's angels to protect Charles and me.

I thought that it was going to be the end, but then I heard a voice of authority say, "Sir, please put your hands on the stirring wheel. And Ma'am, can you please lift your head."

I exhaled and realized that it was cops. I heard Charles exhale as well. I lifted my head up to see a cop staring at me through the window. I heard him tell the other cop.

"Yes, it's her."

"Ok, Sir, can you please roll the window down?" The gun that Charles had was visible and the first cop immediately pulled his weapon out of his holster.

"Gun!" the first cop yelled.

The second cop then pulled his weapon and pointed it at me. Charles then began to explain his weapon.

"Officer, please, I have a permit for my gun. It's in my glove department."

"Yeah, sure you do… and I'm Moses."

"Officer, please listen to me. I'm not joking. It's in there."

"Com' on Hank, let's just do him."

"No, Bill we can't do it right here."

"I want to just look at him die," said the second cop.

"No, Bill we can't do that right here and now. Get them out of the car."

"Charles, what's going on? What are they talking about?"

"Ma'am, please don't say a word. We are going to get you out of here to safety."

"Look Officer, did Captain Haynes send you? We are fine. Nothing is going on, "Charles repelled.

"Look, I'm getting tired of that one talking. I'm about to do him in!"

"Bill, just cool it… alright!"

Charles and I both knew that something was definitely wrong about this situation. Both cops had their guns drawn and pointed at us. And neither one of them wanted to investigate the permit that Charles said he had.

"Charles, these cops are paid by Joshua… let's get out of here!"

Charles quickly started the car and stepped on the gas, but not before a round from the cops' guns went off. The bullets blasted between us and one of them hit the glass next to me and shattered it. I felt the glass that went spraying everywhere. The car spun around and sped off in the direction of the pointed guns. They shot another round and this time, the bullets shattered the windshield. The car was out of control and I thought Charles had been hit, but thank God he wasn't. He got the car in control and blasted off. I grabbed Charles' gun off of the dashboard and began to shoot back at the cops. The bullets were spraying back and forth until I hit one in the right leg. I watched Bill fall to the ground and Hank kept shooting until we were out of sight.

Charles was so shocked at me that he exclaimed, "What!?! Who!?! How in the world were you able to do that?"

"Charles, I had to do what I had to do. Those cops were going to kill us. I had to."

I wasn't thinking about what he had asked me, but I was more concerned with Bill being shot by me. Even though it was his legs that I was aiming for, I still felt bad, but good at the same time because I didn't hit anything else.

"Samone. When did you learn to shoot a gun and who taught you?"

"Charles, did you hear what I said? I had to shoot that cop. They were going to kill us."

"Yes, Samone. But did you hear what I asked you? When did you learn to shoot a gun and who taught you?" I hesitated to answer the question, for I didn't know how he was going to take it.

"Um, well… Chico taught me a few weeks ago."

"Oh, Chico. I knew it," he said, smiling.

"Well, it's quite obvious that he taught you well. It shows. I thought you hated guns."

"I did, but now I'm into them. I mean, for my protect… our protection, that is."

"Since when did you get into them?"

"The moment I squeezed that trigger and was able to shoot my target, that's when I knew that guns weren't that bad after all."

"Samone. You are really starting to change memo here. Where is the innocent and caring Samone that I once knew?"

"She is still here but just tired of being run over and not seeing results of the innocent and caring side of her."

"Is that a fact?"

"Yes, it is." While we were in the car, we suddenly heard sirens behind us.

"Charles, could that be them?"

"It has to be… unless they called it in."

"Well, what are we to do? If we pull over, it could be them and we could be shot…"

The crackling of gunshots started to spray. It was the same cops, alright. They had caught up to us to finish the job.

"I have an idea Samone."

"What is that?"

"I'm going to drive to the APD and see if they follow us there. Then we can request to have them investigated by internal affairs."

"It may work, but the problem is how are we going to make it there with them shooting?"

"Well, my love. Shoot back."

He began to speed the car up to 95 miles per hour. I was frightened, I began to squeeze that trigger and it began to ease some of the tension off of me. I began to release all the pressure and anxiety that I had built up inside of me. I wanted to kill them. I wanted them to go away. I wanted the exposure of them to be known to the Captain. We made it to the APD and to our surprise, they followed us to the station. We got out of the car to make our way into the station when we were directed to get down on the grown.

"Please follow our commands. Get down on the grown and put your hands on the back of your heads."

"Charles, these are not the same cops. Oh My God. We are going to go to jail."

"Ma'am, please don't say another word. For you are both under arrest."

I looked at Charles and he pleaded for my forgiveness with his eyes. I knew that the Captain was going to wonder why I was shooting a gun at his police officers, but the question is… will he believe our story?

CHAPTER FIVE

I was locked up in a cell with three other women who looked to have had been dealt a bad hand in life. They carried on a conversation about how they were innocent and that they were wrongly charged. I couldn't for the life of me figure out why I was in here with them. I told the Captain our story and he had us locked up. He told us that his officer was injured because of me and that I would serve the maximum imprisonment. He didn't show any sympathy and he took their word over ours. I couldn't get a word out until he asked what my dealings with Joshua were. He begged for me to tell the truth about the night of the fire. I refused to and then I was placed in the hell hole.

"So, Ms. Prissy, what are ya' in here for," one of the women asked me.

She had on neon green fishnet stockings with red pumps to match her red skirt. She also had on a black top with the picture of Bob Marley saying, 'Lively Up Yourself.' Her stench was something strong. It was wrong to have such an order about one's self. She smelled of vomit and strong drink.

"I said, what are ya' in here for?"

"I don't want any trouble. I just want to do my time over here in peace."

"There ain't gonna be no peace if you don't tell me what you in here for."

"She's drunk," said the second woman. Her hair was long and black. She was more appealing than both the other woman.

"She's drunk as a skunk. I don't know how we are able to tolerate her stench," the third woman said. All the women were now looking at me, wanting to know the truth of my sentence.

"I'm in here for shooting a cop." Not believing what I said, they all laughed at me and cursed, swearing that if I shot a cop, then they were not prostitutes.

"I will believe it when I see it," the second woman said.

"You won't be able to see, for it has already been done."

"You're such a liar," the third woman said.

"If you shot a cop, then why don't you look like a killer?" asked the drunken woman.

"I may have a look of innocence, but I'm not one to be reckoned with. I have great anger inside me that is ready to burst out at any moment."

All the women then went to the other side of the cell and began to talk among themselves. They did not say another word to me for the rest of the night.

The next morning the officer came to the cell and announced that I was free to go.

"Hey, you gonna take us with?" the second woman asked.

"Where I go, you do not want to go. It's not safe where I'm going." The women looked at me as if I were a stranger to their kind.

"Girl, you gonna need some help when you get out there," said the third woman.

"I'll be okay, but thanks for the offer." They then went back to take their seat in the cell.

"Officer, can you tell me who bailed me out?"

"I did," Brian said, coming into the detainment area. I was surprised by his arrival, for I thought it would be my sister to bail me out.

I stood staring at him; he then said, "You are welcome, Samone."

"Oh, thank you. I thought I said that." The bailiff made me sign release forms and Brian escorted me out.

"I have something for you." I looked at him and then back at the pavement.

"What's that?"

"I have great news. We have set your fiancé free as well."

I looked at him with sincere gratitude and gave him a welcoming hug. He was startled by the sudden change in my demeanor.

"I've been waiting for a hug from you for a while now. I still feel the same about you Samone, but I respect your decision in choosing Charles. I don't know why you have chosen him, but hey, who am I to argue?" I let go of his embrace and felt an urge to just dismiss what was said and start over.

"Look Brian, I have only three words that I can say about this situation and they are I love him. I don't need to explain my reasons. Just know that they are well into him. I do thank you for your generosity in helping the both of us. That was such a nice thing to do." The sudden tension made me want to change the subject to a more relaxing one.

So, I then asked him, "Where have you been? The last time I seen you was in the hospital, the place in which you decided to tell my sister of our kiss." Brian let out a sigh, which let me know that he wished I wouldn't have asked such a question.

"Well, I took off to go to Chicago, Illinois, to do some research for my case. Seems to me that there are a lot of unexplained things going on with you."

An unexpected drop in my spirit let me know that this man was questioning my actions and dealings with his case. He knew something.

"What do you mean?"

"Well, we will have a later date to discuss a case that has now come up. I'm over this case as well and it entails you."

"What about me? What? Am I a suspect?"

"Yes, you are. Your name is written all over the case. Luckily, you have me as your attorney. I know you are innocent; I just need proof."

"What proof is that?"

"I need to know that you didn't kill Joshua Franks. You see, Captain Haynes is sure of your involvement with the murder and now he is going full force with investigating his suspicion of you."

"And what are your suspicions?"

"I already told you, you are innocent."

As we existed the building, I saw Charles standing with Captain Haynes. Captain Haynes's expressions were unsettled and clinging at the circumstances.

"Look here Samone, just because you are free right now doesn't mean you won't suffer the consequences of your actions. You stole that man's money and now you have been accused of killing him. You are a detestable person to our society and I'm going to prove it. May God look at the sins of your soul!" With that, the Captain turned his head and left my presence.

I was so in awe at the words that he said that it made me quenched with fear. I was going to go down for the murder of Joshua. They think I stole his money. From an outsider looking in, I could see how it looked. But the story was not so.

"Charles!" I exclaimed. He grabbed me in his arms and kissed me passionately.

"What about the accusations of the dirty cops?" I looked from Charles to Brian, who was staring at our embrace.

"Well, proof was given to the Captain to show that they were indeed on Joshua Franks' payroll. They had no clue that I had all the paperwork to prove it."

"Thank you, Brian. If there is anything that we can do, let us know," Charles began.

"Of course, there is one thing."

"What is that?"

"Tell me what happened to Joshua Franks. No one knows where he is." Charles looked at Brian with fierce energy.

"I don't know, Man. Maybe he was burned in that fire." I could tell that Charles was holding something back, but I had no clue what it was.

"Yeah, okay Charles. I will take you at your word, but I have proof that says different. I have proof that states that he may still be alive."

"What!?! What do you mean he may still be alive?" I asked.

"Don't tell me she doesn't know the truth?" Brian taunted towards Charles. Charles stood in between us with the answer to the question.

He looked at me and said, "Samone, I'm not sure what to tell you. From what the newspapers say, there was a fire and I assume he died in it."

Charles knew exactly what he was doing. He did not want to convict himself of a crime and wanted me to do the same. His eyes told me what to do next.

"Brian. What news or information do you have."

"At a later date Samone. Go and be with each other. Get your evidence and your thoughts together, for you will need it." Brian got into his car and drove off; I was left behind with a man that hasn't been totally honest with me.

"I hope you don't mind, but I called your sister and asked her if she would come and pick us up since my car is not in the best of conditions."

"Yeah, yeah, yeah… whatever! What I need to know is was you honest with me about Joshua. Is he still alive?" Charles didn't say a word, but his jawbone began to twitch like Joshua's used to.

"Samone, do you really want to know the truth?"

"Yes, Charles, I really want to know the truth."

"Well, the answer is I have no clue."

"Charles, you must know the truth you were there and you took the gun from me. What did you do with the gun?"

Charles stood and listened to my explanation of the situation. I had an urge to carry on with him more reasoning, but my sister pulled up to carry us away.

"Samone, we will have to finish this conversation at my place."

"We definitely will." Dedra had a smirk on her face as we got into the car.

"So, you two are Bonnie and Clyde now?"

"Dedra, could we just cool it with the jokes for right now?" I asked.

"You both are in my car and I can say what I want."

"Thanks for picking us up, Dedra."

"Charles, you are welcome, but to my dear sister… I'm not sure."

"Dedra, are you still upset about that mishap. To tell you the truth if he really loved you from the beginning, he wouldn't have did what he did. I wouldn't have to be pleading a case that has no meaning anymore. You must realize that you are still my sister and I love you dearly."

Dedra drove in silence the entire ride to Charles' place. I guess what I said gave thought to her, for when we got out of the car to enter into Charles' place, she gave me a warm sisterly hug.

"I love you too, Samone. I'm sorry I've been behaving the way that I have. It's just I wanted Brian so bad. And to know that he wanted you over me caused me to lose sight of what you are to me. I'm glad that everything played out the way it did because now I know he really didn't love me from the beginning. You are right." She gave me a warm smile and another hug.

"Thanks Dedra. It means a lot to me that you have forgiven me. And I accept your apology."

Charles stood motionless to the scene he witnessed between two sisters. All that he was able to muster up was a smile and a nod of approval. It was a great feeling to have my sister back in my corner again. For a while, I thought I had lost her. She's such an important piece to the puzzle of my life that without her, my heart consists of a hole. We entered Charles' home, which was now my home. My apartment was now of history. The landlord allowed me to discontinue my lease due to the robbery and because he wanted a feel of security in his apartments again.

"Dedra, I'm glad that you have decided to forgive and put all differences aside because she will need you more than ever. I have no time to just sit and chat about old times, but only time to talk about real issues that are presented upon us now. Your sister is in a world of trouble because of that fool Joshua. It seems to me that he has set her up. I'm not sure what we can do at this point, but I do know I have to go to Dallas tonight to that drop. Something in me is issuing a measure of importance to go."

"Charles, I don't think you should go. If you go, who will be here to help me? I need you."

I stood up and walked over to where he was sitting. He grabbed me in his arms and gave me a hug and kiss.

"Listen, I have to do this for us. This mess has got to be stopped. The drug lords in Dallas tonight will be looking for him to be there. I want to be there to see what will happen when they find out he does not appear."

"What good will that do?"

"A lot, Samone. Just trust him. I think that he will accomplish a lot by going."

I looked over at Dedra to find a concerned expression on her face. She looked like she wanted to add more to her judgment but decided not to.

"I must go with you then."

"No," they both agreed.

"There is no way you are going to Dallas with me tonight. You must stay put in a place where it's safe. Remember, we still haven't heard from the two."

"Charles, tell me, where is it safe? I can't go to Captain Haynes for help. He believes I'm guilty."

"Oh my, Samone, you are in big trouble." My sister's thoughts were not helping the case.

I wanted to go with Charles to make sure he would be fine. Chico was still in the hospital and he had no one to watch his back.

"Charles, you need someone to help you."

"No, I don't. And even if I did, I wouldn't want that person to be you. You are the woman that I love and I wouldn't want anything to happen to you. So you see, you must stay, and besides, you can't leave Austin anyway."

"What!?! You are not allowed to leave Austin? What is going on here Samone? What have you done?"

"Dedra, just calm down. She hasn't done anything but made a foolish decision to love the wrong man." Both Charles and my eyes locked and they didn't move when he continued to answer her questions.

"Who said she couldn't leave Austin."

"Captain Haynes, but he doesn't know what's going on. He is tentative to the facts."

"Would y'all stop looking at each other like y'all the only ones in the room? I mean, this is some serious crap going on here." We both turned our gaze on her.

"We know Dedra. That's why I have to go to Dallas tonight. I have to handle things and take care of your sister."

"Do you have that account number?"

"What account number?" Dedra asked.

"The bank account number that I just so happen to remember by heart, yes, Love, I have it."

Dedra was pacing the floor with a grimace of despair. It was obvious that she had many questions but didn't know how to ask them.

"Look, Dedra, I know you have a lot of questions to ask, but now we really need you to focus on helping. Your questions will be answered accordingly," Charles explained.

"I just don't know. I just don't know what to do," I said.

"I know what. You and I can go to that old cabin that mom and dad use to take us when we were little." Charles looked at Dedra with surprise and welcomed the idea.

"Yes, that sounds like a great idea."

It was a good idea. No one knew where I would be and my sister and I would both be safe. My mother, on the other hand, was still being supervised by the APD. At least I didn't have to worry about anyone getting to her.

"I guess so."

"You guess so? That's it, we are going to that cabin and that's final." I glanced at Charles, who was looking me over and finding reluctance in me.

"I hope you can do some kind of investigation yourself here. I mean, there is a lot of evidence to be shown to the court to prove your innocence."

Dedra looked mesmerized by how Charles and I were speaking in code about my life. She presented us with question upon question till finally, we had to say stop with the questions.

"Do you have a lawyer, Samone?"

"Ummm... well... don't get upset. Brain insisted on being my lawyer since he knows that I'm innocent." Dedra held her composure the best way she knew how, but I could tell that the news bothered her.

"Oh, well, that's good... I guess."

"You guess? He is the best at putting criminals behind bars, but now he has taken this case to prove my innocence... you know he is the best at his job, right?"

"Yes, Samone, of course I know he is the best. I just didn't think you would allow him to be your lawyer after what happened."

"Does it bother you? I will get another lawyer."

"Nah, you're good."

"Well enough about Brian. I'm tired of hearing about the emotions for a man who is no longer in the personal picture."

Charles looked around to notice expressions that left us in silence. And then Dedra let out a laugh and Charles and I followed her lead.

"Why are we laughing?" I asked while laughing.

"I'm not sure, but I needed it," Charles said.

"I'm laughing at the fact that I have a crazy soon-to-be brother-in-law."

"What? What did I do?"

"Don't worry about it. Just know that what you said help me see things from a different perspective. I now can laugh about Brian than cry. Or maybe I'm just delirious…"

With that my sister sat on the couch and was silent for a while. She didn't mumble a word just sat in a soaking deep thought. Brian missed out on something good with my sister, for she is very loyal to those she loves. She proved that by accepting my apology. Even though it's bothering her that I chose him to represent me in court, she took it with a broken ego sympathetic to my needs. Or maybe I was just oblivious to what she was really trying to show me. She was speaking to me through a different method. She spoke to me through her emotions, which all women could relate to. She said through her laugh that she was mad by what had happened to her once impressive relationship. She wanted to be happy once again, but she was too sad to be. I felt bad for my sister. I didn't know what to do to improve her spirit.

"Dedra, are you okay, Sis?"

Dedra looked at me with tears in her beautiful brown eyes and said, "No, I'm not ok as I thought I was."

"Charles, can you give us a moment?" Charles took the offer and went into the bedroom.

"I have no clue as to what you are going to do in the cabin, but know that I will not be there with you. I think I need to get away for a while. This breakup with Brian has left me powerless to how to feel."

"What? I don't want to be up there by myself. And what if something happens to you? I couldn't live with it."

"Don't worry, Samone, I will be up there with you for some days…but not all the time. I forgive you for what you did, but I haven't forgotten how hurtful it is to know that the man I loved dearly loves my sister instead."

"Dedra, what can I do to fix this? I've said I was sorry and that it would never happen again. I keep my word… you know that, don't you?"

"I know Samone, but sometimes a woman has to let the wound heal without the aid of anything." Dedra smiled at me with that gorgeous smile and gave me a hug.

"Oh, Samone, you will be just fine. I will even help you with supplying a rental car to get you back and forth."

She cried a few tears, "Samone, I'm going to let you say goodbye to Charles and I will be back for you in an hour." She stood from the hug and grabbed her keys and purse, then left.

"She is still broken by that, huh," Charles asked while entering the room.

"Yes," I answered with tears.

I knew exactly what my sister was going through, for deep inside, I felt powerless to what to felt about Joshua. I wouldn't let Charles know my real feelings because it was him that I wanted to be with for the rest of my life. And it would only cause confusion if he knew that I was concerned. I only wanted the best for Joshua and me, but he has put me in a predicament that has jeopardized my security in life.

"She has insisted on leaving me alone up in that cabin. She said she would be there for a couple of days, but then she would leave."

"Well, let's get some things together, for she said she would be back in an hour."

"Charles, did you just hear what I said? I will be up there by myself. What am I to do?"

"You are to go up there and have a chance at staying alive. If you stay here, you are doomed to being harmed and I just can't have that. So, get you some clothes and whatever else you need so that you will be ready."

"Oh, Charles, I want to go to Dallas with you. I can be of help and I will be there with you just in case you need someone."

"Baby, I'm going to be fine. Don't you know I already have someone to help me if things go wrong?" I let out a sigh of annoyance and went to the bedroom. I knew that there was no changing Charles' mind, so I left it alone. He followed me into the bedroom.

"Samone, you have to trust me. I know what I am doing. I have been in worst situations before and I have managed to survive with no one. I am a grown-ass man over here, so do me a favor and stop thinking I'm a child." Surprised by the accusation, I turned to him.

"Listen, I've never considered you to be a child… let's get that straight."

"Well, why are you assuming that I can't take care of myself?"

"Charles, I only wanted to help. God forbid something to happen to you. I won't be able to live with myself. You are so important to me and you don't ever realize it."

Once I said those words, my heart sank with sorrow. I began to tear up, but no tears streamed down my face. Charles sat on the bed and relived some stress by exhaling. He put his head in his hands to hide his facial expressions.

"Samone. Come here… sit down right here." He motioned for me to sit next to him on the bed.

"There is something I want to share with you." I stood there motionless.

"Com' on now. Come here."

I went to where he was sitting and sat next to him. He then embraced me and said, "There is no way I want you to ever think that I don't know that you love me. You have proved it by your actions. Yes, some things have happened that I am confused about. But as for your love for me, I feel it and it is real; therefore, I know you do." With that, he stood from his embrace and was silent.

"Charles, I know what I said bothered you, but you have to know that I only want to be with you. I care for your safety just as much as you care for mine."

"Samone, are you almost ready? Your sister will be here shortly."

"Charles, did you hear me. Don't ignore me."

"I'm not ignoring you; I'm just choosing not to comment on what you had to say. Please, Baby, just go to safety."

"I'm ready Charles. I have everything that I will need."

Both of us were exhausted from trying to convince the other that their side was what needed to be addressed. So, we sat in silence on the couch holding hands. I did not want to let go, but I knew the time was coming that we would have to depart from one another.

"Remember, Love, I will always be there for you no matter what."

"I know. Here you go… I think you will need this." I handed him over a piece of paper with Joshua's banking information.

"What is this?"

"That is something you will need to help you. Honestly, I think it will help both of us. Love, don't do anything crazy, okay… and promise me that you will return and be with me for the rest of my life." Charles stood smiling while my sister was outside blowing her horn for me.

"Don't worry. I'm a man of my word. I promise."

We hugged and kissed and as I was exiting the door, I turned back to find him looking at me while holding the piece of paper in his hand.

When we made it to the cabin, it was late. My sister and I unloaded the car of our belongings.

"I'm so glad that we finally made it," my sister said as we entered the cabin.

"I'm shocked that mama kept this place."

"I am to Samone. It looks like she had renovations done to it."

"I wouldn't know. I haven't been here in ages. I'm sure she did, though, for everything looks up to date."

The cabin consisted of three rooms that were upstairs, a living room, a full kitchen, and two baths. According to my sister, my mother had the bathroom downstairs added on.

"Dedra. Where did mama get the money to do this?" My sister looked over at me and shrugged her shoulders.

"I don't know, Sis. I really don't."

We began to take a closer look at the place and realized that every room had its own theme to it. The living room was very simple yet extravagant.

It had modern tables and beautiful plants and flowers to give the room color and life. The couches were made of genuine white leather with mahogany wood, and the floor was dressed with a white bear-skinned rug that appeared to be new. Paintings addressed the walls with such language of many artists. I stood in front of one of the paintings, which happened to be the art of a young Dedra, which my mother was very proud of from the moment she laid eyes on it. My mother used to always encourage my sister to enroll in art school. My sister's passion was not for artwork. She had a talent for it, but she never pursued it.

"Girl, have you gone upstairs yet," my sister asked.

I looked at her and said, "No. Why?"

"You have to see what mama has done up there. This place is nothing like it was when we were children. She has really made this a place where one could reside."

Looking at my sister, I saw the excitement in her eyes to what she witnessed upstairs. I walked up the stairs to find pictures of us when we were kids on the walls of the stairwell. One picture stood out than all the rest. It was a picture of all four of us. My mother had a big wavy fro as well as my father. Dedra and my hair were in afro puffs. We all had genuine smiles that were captured and would last for a lifetime.

I smiled and asked my sister, "Dedra, did you see this picture of all of us?"

"Yes, Girl, I told mama that she did a good job in making us prepared for that picture. I remember dad being upset about his job and mama somehow made it all better. She sure could always make anyone feel better about a situation."

Without my sister seeing my approval of my mother's capabilities, I said, "Yes, Dedra. You are so right about that. She still has the capability today, you know."

"Yes, indeed."

I passed up the picture and continued up the stairs. At the top of the stairs, I found the rocking chair that was in our room as little girls. She would rock us to sleep some nights while reading us a book. She made it a memorable childhood with good memories and I loved my mother for that. It was only when we became older that we appreciated our childhood. Memories of yesterday or years ago for the matter always make me smile inside and out. I have many memories of running up and down the stairs chasing my sister. My mother would yell after us with the words… "YOU TWO SIT DOWN SOMEWHERE!"

After hearing those words, my sister and I would laugh and do it all over again; until finally we would receive punishment for our actions. I set in the chair and began to rock.

"I did the same thing when I saw that chair," Dedra said, smiling as she climbed the top of the stairs.

"I just couldn't resist. Remember the nights' mama would sit us on each knee and read to us?"

"Yes, I remember it like yesterday."

"Mmmph, those were the days. I miss those days when we didn't have to worry about anything."

"I know, right?" My sister walked closer to me and looked down upon me.

"Well, I don't know about you, but I'm starving. Let's go see what's in the kitchen." I didn't realize how hungry I really was until my sister said something.

"Yeah, you are right. I'm starving myself, but why don't you go ahead of me and let me check out the rest of the rooms. Okay?"

"Suit yourself."

My sister turned her attention to the stairs. Before I blinked my eyes twice, she was gone. I stood and walked into the bedroom that was once ours as little girls. As soon as I entered the room, an aroma hit me like that of no other. It was my favorite out of all the fragrances that have hit any pair of nostrils. I engulfed my sense of smell by inhaling what was in the air. I let out the aroma of lavender and felt bad that I had to. Both my mother and I had this thing about lavender that drove my sister and father nuts. They didn't care for the smell but dealt with it on the count of us. I looked around the room and decided to take a seat on the still twin bed that I slept in when I was a child. I was shocked to see that it was still here after finding all my mother's renovations. I couldn't believe that my mother hid this from us. She kept this cabin a secret for us to find out on our own. My mother and I should speak more, but I just can't get over the way my mother sometimes treats me. She has her moments when she can be sweet as pie and other days; she can be as fierce as an angry pit bull.

I used to never see the difference in how my mother treated Dedra and me, but after my mother learned of Joshua's profession, she had a different outlook on who I was. She cared for me dearly, but all the decisions I made regarding Joshua tore her. I could tell she was very bothered by our then relationship. She used to always warn me with the simplest words...

"Samone, Baby now you know that man is going to end up hurting you. You

should get out of the relationship as soon as you can. I love you Dear… and I just don't want to see you end up hurt."

But did I listen? No, I didn't. And now I regret everything. How was I going to make this situation better for all of us? It has to be a way. As I sat on the bed thinking about all my crazy beliefs and young desires, I began to cry. Tears began to stream down my face as I realized that my mother was being so strong for me. She didn't complain when the APD officers took her away. She didn't mutter one word to give me grief in my decision that put her in that predicament.

"Mama, I'm so sorry for what I have done," I whispered. I felt horrible from all the things that transpired.

I knew that I had to finish what was started. I had to, for my mother's sake. I stood from the bed and wiped the tears from my face. As I was about to exit the room, I noticed an envelope with my name placed on the dresser. I wondered what it could be. I reached for it and then heard my sister's voice.

"Samone, come and get it. What's taking you so long up there anyway?"

I didn't return an answer, for I was interested in what was in the envelope. I opened it and I was just about to take out what was hidden in it as my sister burst through the door.

"What's going on in here? Didn't you hear me?" I could tell my sister was getting annoyed by the silence that I was giving her, so I answered her with my own question.

"Did you see this when you came in here?" My sister glanced at the envelope resting in my hand.

"Oh, yeah, I did. I left it there with the intention of letting you find it for yourself." My sister went and set on her twin bed.

"What does it read?"

"I don't know. I was just about to read it when you entered the room." I sat down on my bed across from my sister.

"Read it aloud." I wasn't sure who this message was from... for the writing appeared to be that of my father's. I was willing to wait.

"Dedra, doesn't this look like dad's handwriting?"

My sister's once excited eyes clearly changed with intrigued readiness to learn of what was written. She leaned forward to see the inscription of my name.

"Yes, it does. It's been years since we've seen dad. Why is he now trying to reach out to you or us?"

"You mean you didn't receive an envelope?" Dedra shook her head no.

"I wonder why."

I was now puzzled at the actions my father displayed to my sister by not writing her. It wasn't like him. My father loved me most, but he treated us the same. I remember how we would watch sports together and I would always root for the team he was going against.

He would say, "Now Samone, why you want to bet me to do the dishes? You know your team is going to lose."

He would then laugh and I would join. I miss those days when my father and I were so close. My sister sat patiently waiting to hear what our father left me. I was waiting for her to say something to rush me, but she didn't. I guess she somehow knew that I needed a moment to gather my emotions. When I opened the envelope a piece of paper and a flower head was placed inside of it. It read:

Samone,

Hello, my Darling. I miss you and your sister terribly. I wish I were there to see how my beautiful little woman have grown. I hope you can find it in your heart to forgive me for what has been done. Our relationship has died and I would like to spring it back to life by watering it with words of knowledge of what went wrong. I'm writing you now because I think you and your sister are now wise enough to make a sound decision on whether or not you would like me back into your lives. I hope with all of me that you will let me in. You have to know that what I say is really true and I have no reason to lie. Your mother is the cause of our divorce. Of course, I have fault by not staying and trying harder, but I just thought it would be better for all of us if I left. I hate that I left you two the way that I did, but it was needed. After I found out Denise was in love with someone else, I had to leave. I was crushed. We had both discussed staying together until you two were old enough to understand, but I couldn't face her. It wasn't love that was being given and received. Over the years, I realized that you two were supposed to be my world, but I resented having you two by her. I was angry, hurt, and confused. I tried to be there for you, but your mother insisted that I stay out of the picture. She would always tell me that you two were getting along in life without me. I didn't know how to approach a 9 and 7-year-old with grown-up complications. So with that, I ran. I'm here now and willing and ready to do anything to get you two back into my life. I'm not sure if I can forgive myself if you answer me no. I have lots to catch up on and I want to know everything that is going on. I have faith that you two will love me once again. I have faith that there is hope in us. Let's not waste time. Write or call me back soon.

5523 Rosewood Dr.

Greenheart, MD 72231

My phone number is (552) 555-2697. You can call anytime. With much love and hope...I will desperately wait.

Your Father,

Samuel

We sat in a long dreadful silence. It was a silence that was awkward for the both of us. My sister sifted in her seat before I cleared my throat of challenging emotions that I was trying to hide.

She broke the silence, "I can't believe him blaming mama for everything. He had a choice and he chose the easy way out."

I wasn't so sure how to judge the letter, the words in it, or how to even handle it, for that matter. My father really laid something on our minds to consider. I could tell that my sister wasn't going for it. She had already made up her mind that she was going to dismiss the words given. I couldn't imagine expecting different. She was my mother's daughter and I my father's. I truly loved both my parents, but when my father left, I became a different person. I resented the fact that he left us and my mother didn't make things any better by talking down about him. She would say such hateful and mean words that it tore at both my sister and I. Deep down, I never believed what my mother said about my father. I always felt that she was hiding something from us. And now I knew what it was and why she hid it.

"Dedra, I'm not sure what to say about this letter. I mean, if you think about it… it explains a lot about our childhood."

Dedra didn't say anything. She sat and soaked in the thoughts that began to go through her mind.

"Mmmph, you may have a point. I wasn't going to say anything because I love mama and I just can't imagine her doing something like that to us."

"But she did, Dedra. I'm not saying what dad did was right, but mama had something going on. I remember her on many occasions leaving the house and telling me that I was in charge." Dedra lifted her head so that I could see her eyes.

"You remember that? I was so young."

"Yes, Sis, I remember a lot of things that happened." She smiled a depleted smile and exhaled.

"I remember too."

"I think we should just think about it before we dismiss dad." Dedra didn't respond; she gingerly stood and walked to the door.

"This is something you need to think about. I am already my mother's daughter." With that, she turned away from me and walked out the door and I was left alone again.

Both my parents somehow deserted me. I felt like an outcast. My mother sometimes treated me like a stepchild and my father left me while I was just a child. But after reading from my father, I had made up in my mind that I was going to reach him. After reading the letter, I didn't have the gumption to go view my parent's room. A lot ran through my mind as I stood to follow after my sister to go downstairs. It was a stretch of hope to build things back together again, but it was something worth doing. I needed some sobriety in my life at this time and I had planned on getting it. My father was the key out of this. He would for sure know how to help me. At least that's what I told myself.

CHAPTER SIX

That night I found my sister asleep on the couch. I decided not to wake her, for she seemed to be in a comfortable rest. We talked for hours in the night before we drifted off to sleep. Dedra wanted to know more about the lies mom told. She wanted answers that I couldn't give. Regrettably, I asked her a question that had us in uncomfortable silence for a while.

"Dedra, do you think you could stay with your husband if you found out he loved another woman?"

She looked at me with disbelief and answered accordingly, "Have you forgotten about Brian? I did love him. Do you see me with him?" I bit my tongue.

"I'm sorry. I wasn't trying to disrespect you. I was only trying to get you to see dad's situation. I'm so sorry."

She soon exhaled and told me, "What's done is done... can't change it now."

I guess I hit a nerve because she began to wonder about dad out loud after that. I wanted to keep the peace. So, I admired her thoughts and wished along with her. After what seemed like days, we went to bed. I thought a lot about my father. He was strictly on my mind. I thought about how awesome it would be to rekindle what we once had. I knew in my heart that Dedra would give in and accept him. Everybody makes mistakes and my father is no different.

Just before I went to bed, I asked God questions. I know some people think that you should never question God, but why not? I mean, he has all the answers, right? Isn't it logical to go to the source of all things? 'Heavenly Father, if you are listening, I need answers. I'm not in any way trying to disrespect you, but only ask much-needed questions to get results in my life that will be worth living for. I need to know what will happen to Charles? What is to happen to my father? Can we again have that once adorable love between father and daughter? Has my sister truly forgiven me for what I've done?' After I asked the questions pressed upon my heart, I felt a sweet and safe presence overshadow me. It was so strong that I became frightened by what I felt. I had to speak out and call my sister's name, for it was as if God had come down from heaven just to answer my questions. I could not move. I soon heard a voice that spoke my name. Samone, I am here to answer the questions that were heard.' As this soothing but yet, stern voice spoke to me, I began to wonder if I was dreaming.

"Dedra, come help me."

"Samone, why do you believe you are dreaming? You are being liked by the heavenly father. You have reached his heart and now you are heavenly heard. You should be happy that you are chosen to do something special." As I lied there listening to promises that were spoken to me, I felt a hand press against my shoulder.

"Samone, wake up. Are you okay?" Dedra began to convincingly shake me till I opened my eyes.

"Dedra, thanks for helping me…I heard God speaking to me and it scared me." As I spoke to my sister, I was panting for air to reach my lungs. She looked at me, concerned.

"What do you mean you heard God?"

"Dedra, please listen to me and believe what I'm saying. I heard God speak to me." My sister was amazed at what I was saying.

She then replied, "What did God say?"

"He told me that I wasn't dreaming and that I had reached the heavenly father's heart and I am now being liked by the heavenly father."

"Really?" I exhaled.

"Dedra, am I going crazy?"

Tears began to form in the corner of my eyes. My sister stretched her arms for me to accept the invitation for a hug. For some reason, I felt safe and not alone. She secured my thoughts of not being crazy.

"Samone, I think it's awesome that God has spoken to you. And to even be considered liked by him is extremely beyond imaginable. I think you should really consider opening up to him. I wouldn't mind being in your position." I took in her words and thought to myself, maybe she's right.

"Dedra, the presence of him was so peaceful and soothing. He felt so strong that his presence overtook me. I don't know how to explain what I felt, but I'm concerned. Everything that I've come to believe about my mental health has been involving God. He has been calling me. And I have been running. But in all this, I feel as if my mind has been a rebirth."

"Wow, I don't know how to approach what you just said to me."

"Deep inside, I know it's only God working in me, but to others, I'm considered crazy, wacko, insane, unstable… the list can go on and on. But honestly, people don't know how God can use you. And what happens when He do."

"Samone, listen to what you just said. You are not a crazy, wacko, insane, unstable person. People give labels when they don't understand what they have witnessed. I don't think you are crazy. I think you are specially used by God Himself."

My sister and I shared very intimate life experiences. Some things I never knew happened to her. After the conversation ended, I felt impressed that I had experienced the presence and heard the voice of the only begotten Son of God known as Jesus. Dedra went back to bed after the conversation. I laid on the couch listening to the still sound of the night along with my sister's rhythmic breathing. I thought about the words that were spoken between my sister and me. I loved the fact that she knew exactly what to say when I needed to hear words of encouragement. But as I began to drift off, I remembered something... I got up from the couch and went upstairs to my room. Once I was within my room, I started to reach into my bag for the prescription that was prescribed for me. I popped the pill and told myself that this would take care of all the delusions and reputation of being crazy. Deep down, though, I knew that what I experienced was real... and what was said was too believing for the presence of God was undeniably intense and the words were powerful. I lied down in my bed and prayed out loud... *Dear Heavenly Father, please hear me; please recognize my voice, for it is Yours I seek to learn.* Instantly, I again heard a voice that spoke to me. This time I was different. I deliberately decided to listen without fearing what would happen to me. I knew that if harm were intended for me, it would happen regardless of whether I answered or not.

"Samone, I have answers for you to know for which you have prayed. Charles loves you, but beware of the things that are going on, for his actions are not recommended for you. I have heard many prayers from your father. He is very concerned and wounded by his actions of the past. Soothe his heart by reaching and caring for his love. I am not going to hurt you in any way, for I am the Only Begotten Son of the Heavenly Father. I sit on the right hand of the holder of your being."

I felt pleased and without knowing it, I said, "Thank you for hearing me, for many are not." As I laid there, the security that I felt had faded and the comforting words lingered within me.

Morning announced its arrival with the morning sun. I found my sister in the kitchen cooking up some breakfast.

"Good morning Sista," I said. She looked at me and smiled.

"Hey Sista and good morning. And as you can see, I'm making breakfast."

"Yeah, the aroma is passing through my nostrils." We both shared a little laugh.

"Hey Samone, I was thinking about what we talk about before you left me in that living room by myself."

"Aww, Sis, I'm sorry. I went upstairs to take my prescription and fell asleep. What are your thoughts about last night's conversation?"

"Well, I thought about what you said regarding dad. I've really been back and forth about him trying to come back into our lives. I feel focused on not allowing him back in, but a part of me wants him to. I need clarity on his reasons of leaving. That letter he wrote is just not enough."

"I understand Dedra; I feel the same way somewhat. He did a number on us, but I still want to know him. He missed an enormous amount of time in knowing us. So, let's give dad a chance, okay?"

I arose from the barstool and walked over to the stove where my sister was wrapping up the last touches of breakfast. We embraced a quick moment and I returned to my seat.

"You're right Sis, let's do it."

We set down at the table to eat and we had a very trustworthy conversation. I meant every word I said to my sister. She was someone I looked up to and admired for all the troubles of her life.

After breakfast, I cleared the table and went upstairs to find my sister packing her belongings. My sister knew my thoughts from my facial expression.

"Samone, I have to get back to work tomorrow. It's been a week and that's about all the time I can spare without losing my job."

I hated the truth of the matter, but I knew that she was right. She had to make her living and continue on with her life.

"I understand, Dedra, but I really hate to see you go."

"I know. You know I will return on the weekends." She unexpectedly stopped her packing and faced me.

"I don't want to be here all alone, Dedra. What will I do?"

"Samone, you have to. In order for you to be safe and allow me to have a piece of mind, you have to stay here. Don't you want to please both mom and I, and even Charles for that matter?" I took a seat on her bed then exhaled.

"Yeah, you're right. I need to just stay focus and figure out a way out of this mess. I know Michelle and Tyrone are looking for me and so is the Captain. I can't believe my life has come to this point of running away."

"Yes, I know," my sister said, taking a seat next to me. She embraced me within one arm and continued, "as long as you stay here and don't make a move on your own, you will be alright."

We saturated in silence but were able to hear the television downstairs. We heard someone say the name Brain Johnson, so we instantly jumped up from our place on the bed and flew down the stairs. When we made it to the living room, we saw a familiar face on the screen. Brian Johnson was pleasant for any pair of eyes to witness and he knew it. His million-dollar smile hit home to my sister, for she let out a soft sigh.

"Is this okay for you, Sis?"

My sister turned her attention to me and exhaled, "Don't be silly, of course, it is." We listened to what the assistant district attorney had to say.

"As of right now, the case involving Joshua Franks continues. There have been some discrepancies as to whether Mr. Joshua Franks is alive and well today. In recent activities, there was a fire at the estate of Joshua Franks. His body has yet been identified, but a female witness with a child questioned for the actions taken place during the ordeal. I am well aware that some things have to be answered and I will work relentlessly at solving this case." With that, the news anchor reappeared on the screen with a bright smile.

"Thanks, John, for that story. I'm sure ADA Brian Johnson is working persistently at the case at hand."

We were both sitting and Dedra decided to break the silence, "Samone, what does he mean about Joshua's body not being identified? I thought he was supposed to be dead."

I looked puzzled at the question, for I knew not the answer. An overwhelming feeling came over me as I began to think about the possibilities of Joshua still being alive. The last time he saw me, I had a gun pointed at him and his child's mother. I couldn't explain the feeling that I was currently feeling. I had more dealings with the man who had my mother in the trunk of his car. I had more to do to him for all the damage he had done to my family and me. My thoughts then turned to Charles. Had Charles let the man go free? Had he been lying to me all this time about the state of Joshua? I wanted answers. I needed answers and I was for sure about to receive them.

"Dedra, I don't know what to think of Joshua right now. He should be dead right now. I'm not sure what's going on, but I know who does." Just as I was about to leave the room to retrieve my cell phone, my sister grabbed my arm.

"Just let it go, Samone. Don't dig into it." She pleaded with me with her eyes and how could I reject her.

I sat down and exhaled. So desperately, I wanted to go and dig deep into this nonsense that was spilling. I wanted to find out if Joshua was still alive. I wanted to see if Chico was alright. I even dared the idea to gain information on the people that I was running from. I wanted all this information to agree with the ideas and facts that I already knew. She was looking at me and she knew I was in deep thought.

"What are you thinking, Samone? I know you are trying to come up with an idea."

"Why would you say that, Dedra? I'm just relaxing."

"Yeah, right, Sis. I know that look from anywhere. Samone, promise me that you won't go and do anything foolish while I'm gone. I mean, you know I have to get back and I'm afraid that you are going to do something that you will regret later." Reluctantly I decided to agree with her; I promised.

"Good, now I feel better. While you are up here, the point is for you to be in safety from all those nuts and losers."

"I know Sis; you don't have to worry about me. Even though I know

I'm going to go crazy up here…"

I started to laugh, but my sister cut in and made me stop, "Hey Sis, you are not crazy just a little special, that's all." We both stared at each other before we let out a healthy laugh.

She went back upstairs to finish packing all that she had brought. I wanted to be selfish and hold my sister hostage from the world, but unfortunately, I couldn't. I wanted us to continue with the very deep conversations and open up as sisters should. Inside I hid from my sister my true intentions to find out what was going on back home. I wanted to be in the mix of everything. How could she expect me to just be silent and not make any contact with anyone? Only God knew how long I was going to take for this whole ordeal to pass. I watched as my sister put all her personal hygiene products in her bag.

She then said, "Alright, all done." Dedra turned her attention to me.

"I know you must go, Sis, but I really don't want you to."

"I know, Samone, but the bills have to get paid somehow."

I agreed, "Yeah, you're right." I grabbed a couple of bags from her room and followed her down the stairs.

"I really hate to leave you here by yourself, but you will be okay."

"If you say so, Sis."

We packed the car nice and tight and gave each other a nice big hug. She and I exchanged words of comfort and she was gone.

I entered the lonely cabin after watching my sister turn the corner. I was officially alone. After having the conversations that my sister and I had, I wasn't so sure if I wanted to be alone. My mind began to race and wonder about different people and things. I missed Charles and wanted to see Joshua one last time. I couldn't put my finger on this one thing that my mind began to contemplate upon. Where was Joshua? I had a strong feeling within me that was telling me that Joshua was alive and well. But I knew what Charles told me. He said that he was taken care of. What did that really mean? I grabbed my cell phone off the table and stared at it in my hand. I wanted to call Joshua's old cell phone number but didn't. I dialed all of Charles' numbers except the last two numbers. I hung up the phone and sat down on the couch. I remembered I made a promise to my sister and I was going to try and keep it. Just as I turned on the TV, the phone vibrated within my hand. It was an unfamiliar number. I usually didn't answer calls such as these, but I decided to go ahead and answer the call.

"Hello."

"Yeah."

"Um, excuse me. Who is this?"

"Bitch you know who this is. Or are you that stupid? You thought we forgot about you or something? You owe me something and I suggest you give it up, or you know what's up."

"Look, Michelle, I have no time to talk to you. Do what you have to do. I am not scared of your threats… for that's just what they… just threats."

I didn't hear the foul language that I was beginning to get used to. I heard heavy breathing as if she were disgusted at what I had just said. She was about to say something when she was interrupted by a male who was in the background yelling words of profanity. I was so disgusted that I hung up the phone. I questioned myself as to why I listened that long. I was waiting for the ring back and when there wasn't one I decided to finish what I started a while ago. I dialed Charles' number and when he answered, my heart skipped a beat. I was so excited to hear his voice, but it didn't sound like himself.

"Charles, is everything okay?"

"Of course, my Love, I just miss you so much. I wanted to come and see you but knew that it wasn't a good idea."

"I thought you were going to call me and let me know how things went. It has been a week, you know?"

"Yes, I know. It's just things are going crazy around here. I'm really lost without you beside me."

By the sound of his voice, it sounded as if the words were rehearsed. This Charles was not the man that I had fallen in love with.

"Baby, are you sure everything is fine?"

I guess he was irritated with me asking him about his mood, for he let me have it, "Damn Samone, I told you I was okay. Why you keep asking me the same question?"

I didn't know how to respond to his question, so I held the phone to my ear without saying another word. But honestly, I wanted to just say something that I would probably regret later.

"Samone, I'm sorry, Baby. I'm just under a lot of stress. Too much is going on here."

My silence had softened the hard reality that I was not the blame for the misfortunes of what appeared to be going on. When I didn't say anything, Charles asked a simple question that I could not silence.

"Samone, I know you are still there because I can hear you breathing. Do you know what you gave me?" I had no clue what Charles was speaking of, so I inquired about the invitation to discuss the topic at hand.

"What are you referring to Charles?"

"Do you know what you gave me? That account number that you gave me… well, let's just say it has screwed up some of my plans. I can't get into detail about why but I have to acquire some assistance with this situation now. I know you don't know what it is and how important it is to the ADA, but it's a dangerous topic."

"Oh My God, Charles. What's going on?"

"No need to ask questions, Samone. Just know that Captain Haynes is still on the hunt to sabotage my plan for freedom for both of us. He has been conducting a search to find out more about our case. Hopefully, he runs into a dead end and has to dismiss the charges put against us."

"Charles, what about the bad cops? Are they still around to put things in the Captain's ear?"

"I don't know. But more than likely, they are. Just be strong, Samone and hold on there. I know you want to know what's going on here, but I think it's better for you not to know everything. The more you know the more accountable you are for responsibility." Charles let out a small chuckle and it made me feel a ton better about the situation.

He was right. I wanted to know everything, but there was no need for me to know everything.

"Charles, when will I see you again?"

"It won't be that long, my Love. Just a few more days to a week, you will be free."

"Okay Josh…" I didn't realize how much I was in thought about Joshua, for I almost called the love of my life the name of the man that he killed.

"Samone, my name is Charles. I'm not Joshua. Are you okay? Have you taken that medicine?"

"Charles, I'm sorry. I didn't mean to call you that. It's just...right before I called you, I received a phone call from Michelle and crazy Tyrone....and they always make me think about Joshua. And for your information, I have been taking my medicine."

"Well, that's good. I apologize to say such things. I know you are sensitive to that subject, for you never discuss it with me. By the way, what did those crazy nuts say?"

"Michelle told me that they have not forgotten about me and that they are still waiting on what I suppose to be giving them."

"Oh, really? What did that fool Tyrone say?"

"He said something along the lines of I'm going to take care of her."

"What!?! How long did you stay on the phone with them?"

"...about a minute. Why?"

"Because Samone... they can trace your call and find your location. I can't have that. I'm almost to the point where I'm about to go mad. I need for you to stay at that location no matter what."

"Charles, I have no way to leave now that Dedra is gone. She had to go back to work." There was a pause before he responded.

"Oh. Well good. This will help ease my mind to know that you are safe. Because the last time you acted on impulse and thoughts to help me... you ended up in danger. And I can't have that." There was another break between words being exchanged.

"I know Charles. I'm really sorry about that. I don't know what took over me. But I'm good now."

"I hope so. Well, Samone, I have to get back to the house and finish up.

I'm glad you called. Just stay well, my Love…"

"Charles, I don't want to let you go. I'm alone up in this place and I'm missing you."

"I miss you too, Love, but I have to go. And I'm never letting you go. You are with me and I will be with you forever always."

The words just flowed through the mouth of Charles so easily. I smiled, I felt adored and he left me feeling the joy of being in love with him.

"Charles, I love you. You be careful and just listen for me when you feel like you are going mad."

With that, Charles said other words and then ended the call with repeated words of I love you. I really wanted to know what was going on with the trip to Dallas, Tyrone and Michelle, Brian Johnson, and the Captain. I haven't heard from my mom in a while, but I thought not to call her due to the police watching over her. I just hoped Dedra wouldn't be bombarded with questions regarding my whereabouts. I wanted a lot of things. Heck, I need a lot of things, but what kept me from it were answers. I needed all my questions, thoughts, concern, stresses to be answered.

After the nice meal that I made for myself, I sat on the couch and flicked on the stereo and heard the sounds of Maysa soothing everything that embraced her as her voice exited the speakers. I knew that song that was playing. I began to sing along with Maysa. I wasn't all that good at singing, but it helped me release stress and paranoia. I wanted to escape the reality of life for a brief moment and have someone else's problems, but then there is always someone in worst situations than that of my own. I soothed myself with melodies of love and persistence in the desires of being with the one I loved. I knew that with time I would be with Charles. I knew in my heart that he would soon be in my arms. I wanted so desperately to be with him, but instead, I was here alone. It was a little after 7 o'clock and I needed to just relax and wind down for the night. There was nothing else to do but think in this setting. The music began to drown out as I sat and began to remember the actions I displayed when I went to Joshua's place. At that moment, I actually felt like my real self. I felt invincible and powerful with that gun. I don't know why but I wanted to feel that way again. I felt the tension and fear in the air that night. I knew people wanted to attack me, but they couldn't because I had the power. Only Charles had the soothing words to talk me out of it. I wondered if he really did go through the whole ordeal of killing Joshua like he said. After I sat soaking in my thoughts for a while, I decided to change into my nighties. As I closed the draws to the dresser, I saw my father's letter. I sat in my chair and began to re-read the letter. I smiled as I dialed the number to my father.

"Hello."

"Hello."

"Yes, may I ask who is speaking?"

"I presume this is my father. This is Samone." There was silence we shared as he began to speak.

"My God. Samone. I can't believe you called."

My father seemed to be sincere with his words which made me so excited inside. I was ecstatic to hear from him.

"Yes, it's me. I received your letter and then decided to call."

"Well, I'm so glad you did. How are you and your sister? I'm so speechless right now, for it has been a really long time since we last spoke."

"I know. Well, Dedra and I are doing okay."

I guess my father was able to discern the unreal statement I had made, for he then replied, "Are you sure? You don't sound okay."

I really didn't want to get into my personal life with a father that has not been there for me. Some part of me was upset, but the majority of me wanted the father-daughter relationship.

"Yes, I'm sure. I'm okay. How about you? What have you been up to?"

He hesitated before he answered, "Oh, well, everything is wonderful. I was able to help myself heal after all the things I went through with your mother. I wanted so desperately to take you guys with me, but Denise wouldn't hear of it...."

"Listen, Samuel, you no longer have to feel horrible about the situation. I understand what went down now. It would have helped to know this information when I was a younger woman, but it is what it is." Samuel understood the comments I shared.

We continued the conversation for at least an hour. It took me back to the days when I wished I could just chat with him and it was now that it was happening. My father told me about his wife, Shelby and his son Brice. He expressed his thoughts on love and how he learned the difference between being in love and just loving. Shelby apparently taught him that being in love was the better of the two. My father wasn't looking for love when he first met Shelby at a convention in Houston, TX. He had been carrying around a broken heart that was healed when they bumped into each other. He told me when he first laid eyes on her, she was the most attractive woman he had ever seen. All the cares of a broken love flew from him as soon as they shared a conversation over dinner. When Samuel told his story of meeting a woman that I was now interested in meeting, he told the story with details: like what color dress she had on, her hair, and her makeup. He told it so vividly that I felt his love for her. It was a nice thing. After the conversation ended, I wondered what Charles was doing and if he was thinking of me. I longed to hear his voice. It wasn't long since I last spoke to him, so I decided not to call.

"...you see silence... it's just you and me." I exhaled and went to pour myself a glass of wine.

I wanted to relax my mind from thinking so much. I needed a break from the constant voices I heard. Was it getting worse, or was it just my imagination? I remembered taking my prescription, so I shouldn't be thinking so much, I presumed. It doesn't matter; I'm going to drink this wine and settle my aching mind.

As I began to drink my wine Laylah Hathaway was playing. She was so soothing to listen to. I pushed my hand through my braids and exhaled again. I began to feel the sensation of the wine in my body. It felt so relaxing and incredibly good. She, Laylah, was speaking to me when she sang "On Your Own." It was like she knew my life and what I was going through. The melody rang through my mind. No pressing thoughts are going through my mind. I so loved the way the mood was set in the cabin, even though I was alone. Just as I was about to turn the music up, my phone rang. The caller id stated a familiar number. I wasn't sure if I should have answered it, but it was too late.

"Hello."

"Hello, Ms. Gray."

"...Ummm, who is this?"

"You sure sound sweet on this evening...."

"I would like to know who this may be. Is it a secret?"

"No, Ms. Gray. I was hoping you would recognize my voice." He let out a laugh.

I really didn't find it funny. I was at my relaxation peak and he was ruining it with this little secrecy game.

"Well, is it still a secret?"

"Ms. Gray. I'm missing you." I laughed this time.

"Com' on now, who is this?"

"Brian."

All the tension between my sister and I quickly entered my body. It became limp and tight at the same time. I wasn't expecting this man to call me. Why Lord? Why?

I got my composure back together and I answered him by saying this, "Brian, why are you calling me?"

"I thought I would check up on my client who may be in a bit of trouble. Com' on now did you know it was me?" Actually, after the laughter, I knew exactly who he was.

"No, I didn't," I lied.

"Why are you lying, Samone? I know you knew it was me," I thought to myself, was he that good on picking up on things or was it just a coincidence?

"Brian. Okay, you got me. I knew it was you after you laughed. Are you happy?"

Brian laughed and said, "My my aren't we feisty tonight. I like that." I sat in puzzlement, for he was reading me like a book he owned.

I knew deep inside that he was trying to pry into my love life without my permission. I just wished I met him before my sister, for I knew deep down I wanted a piece of him.

"Brian. What else do you like?" Before I knew it, those words flew from my lips.

There was dead silence and I was about to break it, but Brian interrupted.

"I like great conversations and many other things. Apparently, I like you."

"Brain, let's not got there. I'm really trying to be good."

"Good Samone? Why are you fighting?"

"Hello, my Sister."

I could tell he thought about this for a while, for he then retorted, "Samone, I understand that I was interested in your sister, but it was really never about her."

"What do you mean?" My mind began to race to Charles.

"I mean, I wanted to know you. I have to be honest, at first, it was about business, but when I saw you, I knew I wanted you."

"But I thought you loved my sister. She means a lot to me and I don't want her to ache."

"You speak as if you have some feelings for me as well. I mean, you are questioning instead of flat-out rejecting me. And I thought I loved your sister, but it is you that I desire." I didn't know what to think or say.

I had been drinking wine, I was feeling lonely, and I wanted some action between the sheets. This man just did not know the temptation he was bringing to me. I was telling myself to be good and be mean, but it wasn't working. He was pressing me to love him. I wondered if I would become weak and do so.

"Samone, are you there?"

"Oh, Ummm, yes, I'm here. I'm sorry, Brian. I can't do this. I'm with someone. You know this."

"Really, Samone? I know you are supposed to be in love with that man, but I'm not sure if you really want to let me go."

"Brian, really? I have to have had you in order to let you go."

"Hmmph, that's a good one."

"That's it."

"Why don't you realize that you have had me for a while? I just don't go after what I want, but I get what I want."

"Why are you taking me to this place?"

"What place, Samone? I'm here."

"No, Brian. You are taking me out of my zone. You are taking me out of my orbit of what I know."

"Samone, Samone, don't you know you need change?" Just as I was about to hang up the phone and rang...

Brian answered my thought, *"He will only love you with love, but it is me that will love with all. Brian was saying all the things I wanted to hear at this time in my life. I needed to see something..."*

"Brian, would you answer me this?"

"Yes, Sweetheart. What is it?"

"Brian, if you love me with all... what will be left for you?" He smiled, for I heard it through the phone.

"Hello."

"Samone, give it time. You will know everything you desire. Know this, though; my all includes me." This time I smiled.

"Hmmph."

I never spoke to someone on this level before. It was different. And I liked it.

"Look, Samone, I'm not going to beat around the bush with you and I'm not going to rush you. I will though, be on your mind, for that's where I want to be."

"Brian, just let me see. I have too much going on right now. And I can't handle more emotions and thoughts." We both laughed.

This thing that we were building at the moment was soft and gentle, like a new refreshing relationship.

"Well, Brian, I must go. I don't know what to do right now. You have me confused."

"Samone, in time, you will work out all the necessary decisions that you must make. But I still remember that kiss. Something happened that day. My world shook."

I melted inside and sat there to intake the enhancing atmosphere, the beautiful feeling I kept feeling inside. He was able to make all the racing thoughts cease and quiet down my love for Charles. What was happening? Who was this man? When I saw him on television and in person, there was no difference in the way the feeling was good. Was it to be misunderstood? I had so many questions to ask.

"Cha... I mean, Brian, what is this? What are you playing?"

"Hmmmph... I see we are a bit confused on what to think, eh? It's okay, Samone; if you and I are meant to be, it will be. Know this, though... you and I didn't meet by accident. It was action-taking with great thought."

Brian did not fall into the jealousy trap I had set up on purpose. He slid right around it with confirmation that he was different. I didn't know where to end this, for I wanted to go there with him.

"Brian, I suppose you think I can easily be taken back by your different approach. You did have me a second… but I have to be strong here. This is becoming too much to bear for me."

"Why would you say such things you don't mean? You don't know me? I have a way…"

"Brian, sorry to interrupt you, but you must know something about me." The silence was the sudden witness.

"What do I need to know about you, Samone."

I was so scared inside, but I had to appear to be strong. I was vulnerable but needed to appear I needed no one.

So, I said the next thing just for desperate measures, "I'm not your typical woman, you know. I'm unique."

"Yes, I know this Samone. So, what are you getting at?"

"Please let me finish. I have something going on with me mentally." Silence was now the enemy. I wanted to hear what he had to say.

"What do you mean? Are you challenged, for I like some challenges?" He somehow took my desperate measure and made it a pleasure.

"What do you mean, Brian?" This time silence was provoked to rest.

We both were itching around the subject. I wanted to shoo him away so I wouldn't have to face the fact of disappointment and heartbreak if I went through it with him. He seemed to not care what others thought or felt. Is this what I wanted? A sick and twisted side of me wanted it to just be about me, but the sensitive and reasonable side of me thought it fairer for all. But it wasn't about that.

"Samone, I sense that there is something going on with you all along but wasn't sure. Your sister mentioned some things about you to me, but as you began to know me... you will find that I'm not here to judge you. I want you."

"Brain..."

"It's okay, Samone. I know. I think I have overstepped my reasons for calling you. Wouldn't you think?"

"No, you got the answers you were seeking. You have yourself on my mind now... so I think you have some of what you want."

"Hmmph. Is that right?"

"Yes, it is so."

"Well, my job is done tonight. I'm on to something else next time. Try to keep up, Samone," he said with sarcasm.

"Really. How I feel right now... I think you should try and keep...."

"Oh Samone, you should watch what you say to me. Like I said, you don't know me."

"Brian, you should be careful coming after me... you might just get something you don't know I have."

"Hmmm... really?" I could tell I got his mind thinking and racing with thoughts, but it was my mind that was so clear and with ease.

"Yes, so I guess you have to go now since you have accomplished your first intention."

"...you really want me to go now?"

The way he conversed with me was totally attractive and sexy. I wanted to see where this would go. We had already been on the phone for a while, but I didn't care.

"Well, are you willing to be honest?"

"I will be as honest as I come." I laughed seductively.

"Are you willing to be on me?" The laughter stopped. I could see that Brian was in my head now.

"Brian, I can't always be on top... but I will always be in the top."

"Really? How he wondered?"

"I like to be on the bottom sometimes to see the top, but I have to be in the top to be able to think on a level of...."

"So, Samone. Do you want to feel something real?"

He just really took me from my thought... he was playing the game of words and seduction right along with me.

"I'm here and you are there, Brian. What can I feel?"

"I have many ways of having someone feel things on a different perspective and level. Will you reach that level... I don't know."

All the thoughts of Charles, my sister, Joshua, Captain Haynes, mom, and Michelle and Tyrone escaped from my subliminal mind. It was just Brian and I. As the reality of what was happening faded, I began to picture us alone in a room and we were teasing each other mentally first to see who would subdue the other with thoughts of love and to see who would last the longest without bursting.

"Brian, I want to go there with you, but you must be honest with me."

"I will be honest as I come. You need to know this...I can't be unreal with you."

"Brian, being unreal and honest is two different things. Do you mean you will be honest?"

"I really want you to go there with me. Will you now taste a piece of me?"

"Okay. I will have what you are willing to share."

"Good. Now that that is out of the way let's pick up off where you left. Do you want to feel me?" I was really tipsy from the wine and I wanted so bad to blame it all on the wine, but really it was a part of me that was being me. A side I did not know. Was Brian correct? Was one of his many ways affecting me?

"Brian, it is in me to tell you that I do feel you. I can hear your breathing method speeding; I can see you smiling; you will enjoy me if I let you."

"If you let me, Samone? Will you let me?" he asked, laughing.

"Seriously, Brian, I want to, but you are deep. It's enticing and rich with flavor."

Brian must have loved the way I was responding to his words and he took the next sentence to another level, "I choose to be deep on certain things, but you have me thoughtful on you. You are appealing to me and I want a sweet simmer of love with you. Are you ready for me?"

"Hmmph. That's good. That's deliciously heard."

"No, I want an answer." Silence became me.

"Well, Brian, look at the time." We both let out a laugh.

"So, are you running from me again, Samone?"

"No, Mr. Johnson. I'm just... desiring to get to know you since it is you that I do not know."

"Yes, you are running. Don't run from me... come to me."

"I am not running. I'm here. I said if I let you... you would enjoy me. Well, enjoy me this night and not rush this."

"Alright. I respect your wishes. But know this... you are giving me a hard time in vain. Tell me, why would you lust after Charles and not clinch love with me?" I couldn't answer Brian at the moment.

He was laying everything on me, it seemed. But in honesty, I knew it was only the beginning. So I answered him the best way I saw fit for the situation.

"Brian, love is a moment spent, a lifetime given, and ultimately a thought shared by two minds. I need to be in love which is more intense. Love is ultimately a feeling, but the reaction to the thought and actions of love is often being in love."

"Hmmph. Interestingly given."

"I think being in love is a true commitment that most do not want to go through. It takes time to develop for remembering it is a thought, but thoughts are processed to be actions."

"You are too much, Samone. I thought you were going to be a simple love, but it's looking like it's more to you than the eyes witness."

We both began to circle around the idea and meaning of love and found out a lot about each other. He was the desperate and anxious type looking for love. And I was hopelessly lost trying to love. Maybe Brian found what he has been looking for in me and maybe I was only lost to be found by Brian. I don't know what will happen between the two of us, but what I did know is that Charles was not going to be thrilled.

CHAPTER SEVEN

It's been a few weeks that have passed and gone. My sister has been able to come to visit me on some weekends but not much. And over the last few weekends, Charles has become distant and seemed reluctant to call. I wasn't sure why the sudden change but it was okay. I found a new friend in my father. Samuel has been keeping me company by phone and we thought it to be a good idea for him to visit. At first, my sister was totally against meeting with her own father, but I had to relax her with words that persuaded her to hear him. My sister could be very selfish and not understanding at times. I wanted Dedra, myself, and my father to have a nice dinner and talk like Samuel and I do all the time. It could be a beautiful relationship if only people would allow it to happen. My father was very excited about the ordeal. He wanted so badly to build back the relationship we all once shared.

Dinner was set on the table when the hourly news report displayed on the T.V. Michael Brock's smile hit the screen with such ease. Sitting next to him was not his normal news companion Janice Calbright. A lady by the name of Jennifer Ashton was now reporting. She had long blonde hair with green eyes. She seemed to be serious about her work, for her demeanor showed it all. I turned the volume up a little to see why Brian was on T.V. They were televising the actions of the ADA. He was working hard to free a certain client of his of all her charges. I sat in that adjusted lazy boy chair, feeling free again. The feeling of being free to experience the other night was returning to me, not void. I went over the said words Brian and I had shared, I began to reminisce on the laughter we encountered and I realized that Brian was a deep, wise, romantic, and I exhaled. Love had hit me again but in a different way. I always wanted to feel that same free feeling, but I didn't know how to break this to Charles without hurting him. Sitting staring at the television screen, I began to wonder which love would do me the most good? I wanted to know which one would cherish, love, and create with me. I wanted to see who would take the most time in getting to know me for me. I adored them both. Charles and his manly ways and his take-charge attitude made me notice the dimples even more. And Brian was much more intelligent with his visible point of view of life situations and other things. Although I thought about Charles' feelings regularly… I also thought about Dedra. I thought about how Brian wanted to go on with us without thinking of my sister's feelings. I wanted him to know that she was a huge reason I would not pursue a relationship with him. He needed to really convince me that he was being sincere. A simple paragraph of loving and sensual conversation was not going to make me hurt my sister more. I hurt her once regarding that good, thoughtful kiss. I'm so back and forth with my feelings on Brian because of my sister; I really didn't want to miss out on a free love… a love doing what we wanted out of good, having romance throughout the whole love we share, and being passionate and honest always. A blissful love is what I think Brian has to offer for me… but for Dedra, it was something else. Love has to have chemistry and I feel as if I have some with both. I'm so baffled. I see something is going on in the air. I mean, I'm not supposed to be struck by love twice at the same time, do I? But for some reason, Charles was distant to me. I tried calling him, but it's as if something is going on. He would not carry with me a thoughtful conversation. I was beginning to wonder about him. Along with my father taking up my attention, Brian walked around to the front door to seek me. I told him that he must talk to my sister and make sure she was good with this. I didn't want to face my sister about this situation. He agreed after some discussion. It took me to give him one of my arms, a leg, and a toe on my last foot. He was not willingly ready to face his former young love. I tried to keep calm, but I desired more for what my sister and I received from Brian. So, he decided it would be a good idea to see what Dedra had to say even though he knew it would be some drama. I could tell Brain knew the "When a Woman Is Fed Up" song by R. Kelly. He knew that she was going to let him have it, but he needed to produce a good feeling between everyone. Would he be able to do this? I'm not sure, but I refuse to go behind my sister's back and date her once true love. Everyone will look at me as a confused young woman... and honestly, I am... I have the two best loves of the world wanting me... and it was in my hands to deal with. I could go either way but was uncertain of which to be with. So, I made a decision that most women wouldn't make. I decided from that night on I would be with both. I know. I know... seems to be very lustful of me, right? But what could I say? I wanted both worlds... my cake and eat it too and to sustain my sweet tooth for both. Is it wrong? I think I love both of them differently but at the same intense level. It took me by surprise that I was making a decision to try and keep them both. Who was this woman emerging from the distances of nowhere? Why was she showing her face now? Why did I want to do something so bad but, in return, feel something so good? I wanted for the life of me to do the right thing. But I was so confused about what to do. I know it's only right for me to share my love with one instead of two, regardless of what I say. I didn't know how I was going to pull this off, but I was willing to give it a chance. I knew that Brian loved but how much he wanted to be loved by me was different.

I was beginning to get cabin fever. I wanted to go out and see things instead of being cooped up in the cabin. From what my sister says, my mom is doing fine and no one has tried anything. Dedra let me know that the captain was still looking to pin trouble on me. She said, by the looks of things, he didn't have enough evidence to put any blame on me. So, instead of going after me, he was now putting his attention on Charles. I asked her how she knew all of this.

She only answered me with, "…because he told me Samone." I wondered what was next for Charles.

I knew Charles was a very intelligent man but was he looking for this to come. Trouble was trying to find its way into my life because the captain knew that if Charles was captured for anything, I might come to his rescue. Apparently, Brian has been working like a busy bee. He was keeping me out of trouble and recommended me to stay put. Brian mentioned that my being absence was very beneficial for him to get things done. He let me know that the suspicious people in his life were on his back about his case. Brian didn't seem like the man that couldn't handle pressure. His statue and resilience of the case made me see that there were people out there that could maneuver in any situation.

Little by little, my life was beginning to get back to normal. But it was far from over because I still had those crazies looking for me, Brian, and Charles, and Joshua to consider. I hadn't heard anything from Michelle or Tyrone and I wondered if they were over the whole ordeal. They couldn't be, or else I wouldn't still be locked up like some criminal in this cabin. I sat down to watch some T.V. and found that there was very little on that captured my attention. I flicked through the channels and thought about my mom. I missed her. I hadn't seen her since that night we found her in Joshua's Lexus. I thought to call, and at first, I wasn't going to, but something told me to. I dialed her number and on the second ring, she answered, sounding half asleep.

"Hey Mama," I said.

"Samone, is that you? I can't believe it. My Baby." I heard the release of pressure come off of my mom. She had excitement and contentment in her voice.

"Baby, the policemen are driving me nuts. I'm bout' to shoot me one of them."

"Aw Mama, what do you mean? Aren't they treating you good?"

"No Samone. They are not. They are all up in my business..." I cut my mother off, frightened that one of them had tried to harm my mother.

"Mama, has anyone tried to hurt you?"

"Oh uh no... Baby, why do you think a cop would try to hurt me?"

"Because Mama, I know things that you don't. I don't want anything to happen to you. This will be all over soon. I promise."

I could understand my mom's privacy. But, having a cop outside your house looking at everyone who comes and goes would drive me nuts as well. I exhaled after thinking about my complaints about where I've been residing. I felt guilty.

"Mama, guess what?" I wanted to change the subject for the subject we were chatting about made me feel sad and hurt.

"What, Baby?"

"Dedra and I have reconnected with our father."

"Oh, yeah, I know about it already. You sound really excited about it."

"Why shouldn't I be? It's been years since we last talked."

"Yeah, I know, Baby. Samone, your sister, told me some things he's been telling y'all. And I can't lie… some of it is true. I never meant to hurt the two of you by keeping you away from him. I just thought that I could handle the whole situation on my own. Now, I realize I was wrong in doing so. I hope you can forgive me."

I sat there thinking about what she had just confessed to. I didn't know what came over my mother to apologize. My mother hardly ever apologized for anything she did. She always considered herself to be right.

"Mama, thank you for your apology. It means a lot to me that you did that. I know it takes a lot for you to do something like that, knowing that things didn't go your way. I accept your apology." Silence became our friend and we both thought of it to be right to keep it.

I didn't know what to think about all the things my dad told us and now how I was witnessing my mother's expression of an apologetic gesture that she had displayed.

"Mama, why did you let dad go? Didn't you love him?"

My mother set on the phone, breathing slightly louder for me to hear. I guess it was the questions that I had asked her that made an upbeat in her heartbeat.

"Samone, I knew the day would come where I would have to answer these difficult questions, but I didn't think it would be now. Samuel and I had testing times and the times between him and I played out. We fell apart. I couldn't find the words to explain to you and your sister that I didn't love your father anymore. And when I met your stepfather Jerome, I knew I had to say goodbye for good. I never meant to hurt your father, but I unwillingly did."

"But Mama, why did you stop loving my dad? I just don't understand?" I was on the break of tears and my mother heard it over the phone.

"Samone, maybe this is not the time to do this. I mean, you have all that stress in your life… maybe you don't need to add to it."

"No, Mama, tell me the truth." My mother hesitated for a minute, but she soon rediscovered her speaking abilities.

"Alright, Samone, I wasn't attracted to him anymore. He gained all that weight and I didn't like it when we were alone. There I said it. Now you know the truth."

I wasn't ready for that one. It hit me that my mother married my dad for looks. At least that was what it sounded like. I didn't want to get into it for the things my dad told me now made sense to me. I pictured why my mother stopped the relationship. All kinds of thoughts entered my mind. I can see how I got screwed up. I could relate to the messed-up decisions I was making and how I so desperately wanted love.

"Okay, Mama." I didn't know what else to say, so I left it at that.

"That's all you have to say, Samone? I don't want to go through this conversation again. So get it all out while you can." I didn't want to press the issue.

My mother was making me angry with the silly decision of attraction being the downfall of my father and her. It sounded petty to me and I thought it was just a bunch of bullshit. I knew my father was on the heavy side growing up, but he took care of us and he loved us.

"Mama, I don't have anything to say right now. That answer caught me off guard and I was ready." I now wanted to exit the conversation and be in peace with my thoughts.

"Well, Mama, I got to go."

"Well, alright, Samone. I gave you your chance. Don't bring this back up to me."

"I can't promise that and I just don't have anything to say right now. Bye Mama."

"Bye, Samone take care and I love you, Baby." With that, she hung up the phone.

I guess it irritated her that I brought up all the emotions of the past and did not open up in a question about it with her. I knew I wanted to know more things. I just couldn't open my mouth to ask her. I thought it was not the truth anyway, but I had to take her at her word. I didn't want to make her angry, so I think I made the best decision to get off the phone with her.

Now that the conversation was over, I was now alone again. Just when I was about to go and bathe, I received a phone call. I answered the cell phone and found out that it was Charles. I've been waiting on really talking to him to find out what was going on with him. I knew something wasn't right.

"Charles, how are you doing?"

"Not good, Samone. I know I've been distant lately and I have my reasons. I want to come and see you. It's been long enough." I smiled with satisfaction, knowing that my man wanted to see me. I was so glad that he said that I let out a giggle.

"Oh, that makes you happy, huh?"

"Yes, it does my Love."

"Well, we have to talk about some things and I want to be in person when I talk to you."

"Uh oh, that didn't sound too good," I thought to myself.

I knew something had Charles uneasy and unsure of his love for me. At least that's what I felt from him.

"What does this concern Charles?"

"Just hold on my Love I'm coming to see you right now. I made it a point for me to go and see you. I've missed you." Hearing those words made a ton of worry ease up off me.

I began to think about him having conversations with Dedra about where the cabin was. I knew they had deeper conversations about things, but Dedra was so secretive about things regarding Charles. I didn't like it one bit. I began to think the worst. Could she and Charles be having a romantic relationship behind my back? Obviously, my sister liked Charles, but she never showed any jealousy or any other thing that should raise my suspicion. I blocked the thoughts out of my mind and turned my attention back to Charles.

"Baby, are you there?"

"I'm sorry, Charles. Yes, I'm here."

"Alright, well, I will be there like right now. Come outside."

"Oh Charles," I almost delightfully screamed.

I hung up the phone and ran outside, finding my fiancé with roses and dimples galore.

"Hey, Baby." I ran down the steps to the cabin and found myself within his arms, and a seductive kiss waited also.

"Baby, I'm so glad to see you. I missed you."

I covered his face with my kisses and he let out laughs of glee. I was so excited by his impeccable timing that I had noticed that daylight was gone.

"Com' on, Baby, let's go in." I took his roses and he followed me inside.

"Baby, I can't believe it… you are really here." Dimples showed me that he was delighted as well. He was showing pearly white teeth.

"I know my Love. I've missed you these last few weeks. We have so much to talk about."

He had me in his arms one more time and kisses began to flow and became heated. He brushed against me and I felt his nature rise to position. We were in the act of making love once again when his phone just kept ringing. I looked across the room and at the phone as if to warn it to shut up, but it kept ringing. Charles then became irritated by it and stopped the thrust that he was giving me. I was very vexed by the notion of this person. I knew they didn't know what he was doing, but they should have realized by the second sequence of calling that he wasn't available.

"I'm sorry, Baby. Let me see who that is. It may be Chico."

After hearing Chico's name, I began to think about questions that I wanted to ask Charles. I wanted to know how Chico was doing.

"Aw man, it's the Captain."

He tossed the phone back on the couch and returned to the floor where I was waiting for him. He took me in his arms as if nothing had happened. I was now in my own world of thoughts and I wanted to know what the Captain could want. I didn't say anything, for Charles made me remember why he was in my arms. Another night of passion and an expression of it was in complete view of my thoughts. I sat up from the floor and realized how soft the bear rug was. It actually had me thinking it was a bed.

"Charles." He rolled over and looked at me with his hand in my hair.

"What's up, Samone?"

"I love the way you make love to me. You take your time and adore my body with every move." Charles lay there with that same excited smile he gives when he is praised for something.

"I love you, Charles Lucas Brown. Thank you for being in my life." Charles sat up and gave me a warm hug that ironically gave me chills.

"I love you too, Samone Gray. And I would like to also thank you for being in my life even after I was being distant. You could have given up on me and told me not to come up here, but you didn't. I don't think I would have listened to you anyway if you told me not to come. I had to see my Samone Gray and be in her arms once again." He gently stroked my back with kisses coming from his soft manly hands.

"I have to tell you the truth. I didn't know what to think about your distant behavior. But I knew that wasn't you. I knew you had to be going through something and that you just needed time to take care of the things you needed to." Still looking at the loveseat, I felt a brush of lips across my shoulder. Charles exhaled and let the air refill his lungs as he inhaled.

"Samone, I know you have been wondering what has been going on. I just wanted to feel you first so that some of these feelings I have could just escape my being." I looked at him and recognized the seriousness he was displaying.

His seriousness made me tense a little, but I tried to stay optimistic about what he was going to share.

"Well, I went to the drop as one of Lester Green's associates. The men at the drop wanted to deal with Joshua only and they all were mourning in some kind of way for his lost...."

"Did you see Michelle and Tyrone there?" I interrupted.

"Just listen to me, Samone and I will tell you what happened." I realized my mistake in sporadically speaking.

"Yes, they were there, but they didn't recognize me. I had on a disguise so that they wouldn't. Tyrone was the man of the hour. Everyone was asking questions and making plans with him that I think it went to his head. Michelle was right by his side. When the men and other women asked where Joshua's cut was, the room became silent. I felt the tension rising between the others and Tyrone and Michelle. Michelle interjected and said we have made plans to include Joshua's cut at a later time, but we have some of the money and coke of our own and we would like to be included in this organization. Some of the men whispered among themselves. The other woman looked over her sunglasses with piercing eyes. She was one to reckon with. I heard her name as being Lady Cruz. And Samone, trust me, you don't want to know her kind. She is dangerous and ruthless to the core. She is up there in statuses like that of Joshua and Lester Green." Charles put my hand in his while he told his story of doom. Charles continued with the story, "one of the men in Lester's crew asked me who I was. At first, I didn't know what to say, but I replied that I was one of Lester's men that worked out of the Northwest side of Texas. I guess the man didn't care, for he started telling me things about what he did for Lester. Turns out he was a lookout for Lester following Joshua's play. Lester Green was apparently making moves that could have given him power over Joshua set. Everyone there respected Lester for what he was trying to do, but they looked down on him and his men for what he was about. Joshua got along with all the drug lords of Texas. He paid them well for their services and Lester Green wanted to pay less. And that's the real reason why they chose Joshua over him. Lady Cruz responded to Michelle by saying that they didn't know if they could trust them. She said that word on the street was that they were trying to take over and that they had something to do with the murder of Joshua. Both Michelle and Tyrone were flabbergasted at the taunting was of Lady Cruz. Tyrone took it upon himself to tell her that they had nothing to do with the murder of Joshua and also that Joshua and him were close and they had no intentions to run Joshua's set. Lady Cruz wasn't buying it, but the others were taking what they had to say easy on the ears."

I sat there listening and the description that Charles was giving made me feel as if I attended the drop. I was all opened eared taking in everything Charles had to say. Charles took a moment to himself and gave me time to ask a question.

"Baby, did they agree to let them in the organization without the money?" Charles saw that he had built an audience with only me listening. He knew that I was listening to every detail.

"You really want to know, don't you?"

"Duh! Yes, I do." Charles let out a giggled and continued with the drop.

"Well, after everyone discussed everything, they saw that Tyrone could be okay with the organization. Michelle was thrilled, for I saw her grip on Tyrone's arm become more. Then someone spoke up from out of Lester Green's set and said we also need someone who can be trusted to do our job. The drug lords then turned their attention to Lester Green's set. One of the men that were speaking spoke up and announced that they had been without a leader for some time and that they had someone in mind to run it.

Lady Cruz asked them who was in mind and for the man or woman to step up to be seen. A man by the name of Lamont Green stepped up. It turned out that this man was Lester Green's son. They began to ask the set different questions and they then questioned themselves upon who knew of him. The drug lords all decided that they could put Lamont on probation to see how he would work. Everyone put all the dealings and business to rest by accomplishing what they came out to do. Everything was done and we were about to go home when a man walked into the room. Everyone looked at the man in disbelief that he was there. Even Lady Cruz was shocked."

"Who was it, Charles? Who was the man?" I wasn't expecting too many surprises after I heard that Michelle and Tyrone were in the organization.

"I don't know Samone. I don't know the man. I never have seen him in my life. At first, I thought it was Joshua or even Lester, but it wasn't. I wondered why everyone was so shocked. I know just about all the drug lords, for that's a hobby of mine to know. So, when I saw this man, I was disappointed in myself. He didn't say anything, but I'm back. And I want my shit back. No one said a thing. I asked the man who had been talking to me who he was and he told me that he was Slim. I came across his name before in my studies, but I couldn't put two and two together. Slim was said to be forced to retire from the game, the man told me. Guess what, Samone?"

"What?" I asked.

"Slim is a politician now. He is some sort of Mayor for a city near Chicago."

"Really?"

"Really Samone. I found that odd as well." Charles read my mind from my facial expression.

"Why would he want to get back in the game?"

"I don't know, but we were all dismissed after he said those words. The big pin told us to carry on with business and that they would get back to us. I remember looking at Michelle and Tyrone when he entered the door and they began to whisper to one another. They seem that they weren't struck by instant conviction as the big pin was. As I passed them when going to my car, I heard Michelle say, *'Yeah, we have to get that money from Samone. We need it.'* And Tyrone agreed and said, *'We need to find her.'* I couldn't grab no more than that, but I now know what they are up to."

Charles sat up straight up on the couch and then reported that he looked into the account and found out money was being wired into it. And it was a constant change within the amount, which meant that someone was overseeing the account. Charles told me that he was about to see if he could impersonate Joshua to see if he could deplete the account but was wise not to.

"Samone, someone from Austin is overseeing that money. I think Brian is on to something. He is investigating the account now. It doesn't make you any safer because your name is on it. You could make some moves with the account if you wanted to."

"Charles, I don't want to mess with that account. Someone may kill me for it."

"Samone, they are already planning on killing you. Your name is written all over it. I hate to be the one to tell you these things, but I would rather it be me than anyone else."

"Oh, Charles. What am I going to do?" I got up from the floor and met him upon the couch.

He took me into his arms and said, "Don't worry, Samone, I got a lead on who it may be." I gently pushed away from his grip without entirely letting go.

"Charles, who could it be?" He looked up toward the ceiling and exhaled the name Joshua.

"What?"

"Yes, Samone, it only makes sense. His name is the only other person, right?"

"Right," I agreed.

"Then it has to be him. I have to tell you the truth now. I left Joshua that night with Chico's men. Some of which I think can be paid off. So, I think Joshua may have paid them off to spare his life. I don't know the truth of it all yet. But that is my suspicion."

At least Charles and I were on the same page when it came to Joshua being alive. I felt it in my gut that he was alive and well. I wondered why he didn't show up at the drop. I guessed he had plans of his own. Both Charles and I were quiet, with soft music playing in the background. We listened to Stevie Wonder's ribbon in the sky. I knew there were much better things to talk about, but I didn't want to. I wanted to talk about something simple now. I was out of the mood to hear negative happenings.

"I love this song." Charles agreed and began to rehearse the song himself.

He actually had a nice voice. He went well with the speakers. I joined and Charles then relinquished his vocal skills. He looked at me and smiled.

"Don't stop, Charles; keep going." Charles took my suggestion and began to sing.

He finished the song and then sat quietly. I knew he had begun to think about all the things that had taken place since he'd been here.

"Charles, let's go upstairs and go to bed."

"No, Samone, I'm not finished telling you everything unless you don't want to hear the rest of it."

"No, Charles, I thought you were done."

"No, I'm not." Charles shifted in his seat. I could tell that he was uneasy.

"What's wrong?" I asked.

"Chico may not make it." My mouth dropped and I couldn't say anything.

But life came back to me and I said, "The last time I saw him he was in good spirits. What happened."

"Well, it's his heart. The doctors said that it's too much stress from his mishap and it's making his heartbeat irregular. They are doing everything to save him, but he was in critical condition when I left him. I don't know what to do for him. I feel like it's my fault." His head went into his hand to hide his face.

"Charles come here," I beckoned, "I know it's not your fault. He will make it through. He is pretty strong." It hit me what Lena must be going through.

"Oh My God, how is Lena?"

"She won't leave the hospital. Both the doctors and I told her that it would do her good to get some time away from the hospital. She won't hear of it. I feel sorry for her because Chico told me that he began to see some hope between the two of them. They use to date back in the day, but they thought it would be a good idea to just remain friends. But in recent events, they decided to try at it again. She is so stressed out. I told her that I had to get some air because it was sickening me to see him that way. She told me that she understood and told me to come back. She would call me when changes were made. She believes in her gut that he will pull through. She expressed to me to just wait and see. And that she was right. I hope she is. I miss seeing Chico up and moving."

"When did this happen? I mean, with Chico becoming critically ill?"

"Oh, let me see," Charles thought out loud, *"It had to have been three days after you left. He's been in a critical state since then. I can't believe it; I may lose the best stepbrother one could ever ask for."* We set in silence for a split second before I came up with another question.

"Charles, how are your parents taking it?"

"Well, his dad is questioning how he even got stabbed. And my mom is taking it pretty hard. She has grown attached to him even though she knows how he is. Chico always treats my mom with respect and good manners."

Charles's shoulders became limp and his head was now looking straight ahead. Charles murmured something under his breath that sounded like I'm gonna miss him.

"Charles, I know it looks bad, but you have to believe that he can recover from this. Charles, don't sit there and think of your friend and brother already being dead. He still has a chance to live. You have to believe."

I took him in my arms and he began to let a few tears drop. I felt bad for him. Emotions started to rise up and I had to suppress them. There was nothing left to be said, so we both sat in tears of despair. I even shed tears with him. We were both holding on to each other and letting tears show up on our faces.

"Samone, he looks so lifeless lying there in that bed."

"Is he on life support?"

"No, not yet, but they were talking about it."

"Oh wow," I sobbed. Charles stood from my embrace and wiped his wet face.

I took it as if he didn't want to look like less of a man because he was crying. It was already too late for that. He already shared with me his sensitive and emotional side. It was nice to see that he had feelings too. I really didn't want to hear any more bad news, so I asked Charles if he wanted to go to bed.

"Yeah, Samone, I could use some sleep, but I don't know if I will get any."

"Well, let's at least try."

"Okay." I took Charles by the hand and led him upstairs.

When we made it to the top, I decided to sleep in my mother's room. I thought since it was one bed, it would be nicer. As I opened my mother's bedroom, I noticed artwork from different artists. A nice huge picture of a family was above the bed. It was a baby in the arms of the mother and the mother was in the husband's arms. They were all naked but nothing graphic for the eyes to see. It was lovely to look upon. I flicked on the light and realized my mother had changed everything about her room. There was a nice king-sized bed with purple and white bedding. In two corners of the room opposite of each, there were artificial plants. My mother had a dresser of cherry oak that matched with the headboard of the bed. I opened the closet to be nosey and found a few outfits my mother left.

"What are you doing, Samone?" I didn't realize that Charles was reviewing the room as I was. He looked over the room as to be impressed at what he had seen.

"Are we going to bed now? Or are we going to look under the bed?" I could tell that Charles was trying to be funny, so I let out a laugh. That brightened the room, for he joined me with the laugh.

"No, Charles. I'm just looking at everything because my mother changed this room to its entirety. So I was just being nosey."

"Uh-huh. Okay." I turned the ceiling fan on and it began to spin.

I noticed pictures of Jerome and my mom on the dresser. They had smiles for days. I jumped in the bed and had Charles turn out the light. When Charles lay down beside me, I felt a presence overshadow us.

"You feel that, Charles?"

"Feel what, Samone?" he responded.

"It's like a presence is in here with us."

"Ah, Samone. Chill out; it's nothing there." Charles didn't recognize what I was feeling or felt. I was lying in bed as Charles put his arm around me. I moved his arm and went into the other room.

"Samone!" Charles yelled. I didn't tell him that I was going to take my medicine. So when I returned, he asked what that was… me leaving him.

"Charles, if you must know, I went to take my prescription."

"Oh. Alright, that's nice." He placed his arm where I had recently removed it.

Charles drifted off to sleep, but I lay awake with the thoughts of Brian. I wondered what he could be doing. Then I began to think about Chico.

What awful news that was for Charles to give me. I sighed. My thoughts began to jump everywhere. I began to think about the drop and about who Slim was. I thought about if Joshua was around doing dirt. I thought about Michelle and Tyrone.

I looked down at Charles, who was sleeping like a baby and I thought to myself, *"he's leaving me up by myself... how could he?"*

As I drifted my thoughts back to my father, mother, and sister, I began to slowly drift off to sleep. I couldn't think anymore, so I finally went to sleep.

CHAPTER EIGHT

The following morning, I woke up to breakfast in bed. Dimples smiled his dreaming smile that made my heart skip a beat.

"Good morning, Baby."

"Good morning, my Love. You made me breakfast. How sweet."

"Yeah, I figured you would need a good breakfast for today's events." I took the fork in my hand and began to pick up eggs with cheese.

"What's going on today," I asked.

"I'm taking you to see Chico. I got a call this morning saying that he has awaked from his coma." Charles beamed with delight.

I became very excited by what he just said to me. I couldn't believe Chico may have been doing better and I was going to see my friend.

"Oh Charles, that's great news! I knew he would come back to us. How is Lena?"

"Lena is doing much better. She told me that she was able to have a conversation with Chico before he asked to sit up. Lena is in good spirits. Dr. Stewart called me with the news. Chico said he wanted to see you to make sure you were still alive." I let out a snicker before I sipped my orange juice. Charles set next to me as I devoured the breakfast he made for me.

"Wow, Baby, you were hungry." Charles looked at me with amazement as I wiped my mouth.

"Yeah, I guess I was hungrier than I thought. I'm glad you thought about me. The pancakes and eggs were delicious."

"Thank you. Now get up and get dressed. Let's get a move on things." Charles took the breakfast tray from me and exited the room.

I got up from bed and channeled my steps to the bathroom. I looked in the mirror at my stitches and realized that they were healing pretty well. I thought to myself, *'I wonder when I need to take them out?'* It was good we were going to the hospital. Maybe I would see Dr. Stewart and he could take them out. I put my hair back in a ponytail to cover the contusion. I went forward with my morning regime as Charles entered back into the room.

"Charles, I think my stitches need to come out. I know the doctor has been looking for me." Charles pushed back hair where the bruise was located. He eyed the contusion and agreed with me.

"We can have Dr. Stewart look at that before we leave the hospital."

"Thanks, Love." I smiled a genuine loving smile that made the dimples suddenly appear on Charles's face.

"Did you eat something, Baby?"

"Yes, Samone. I ate before I woke you." Charles walked past me to enter the shower.

"Samone, did you use all the hot water?!" Charles yelled.

"No, I don't think so. Is it cold?"

"Nah, I just wanted to bother you."

"Ew, Charles, you make me sick." I walked out of the bathroom and put on my white sundress with matching sandals.

I was glad my feet looked to have a fresh pedicure. Charles stepped into the room and put on his boxers, jeans, white shirt, and his white K Swiss tennis shoes. He looked fresh and crisp with the creases in his clothing. Dimples brushed his hair and asked if I was ready.

I replied, "Yeah, I'm ready."

"Let's go." When I made it downstairs, I noticed that the living room was straightened up and it smelled as if someone had done some cleaning.

"Thanks for cleaning, Charles. It needed it."

"You are welcome."

It was already hot when we made it outside. It was only morning, but it felt as if it was noonday. We jumped in Charles's rental and he put on the air.

As the air began to cool, I said, "Too bad those cops messed your Impala up. Now you have to get another car." Charles didn't say anything at first. He looked straight through me.

"Charles, are you okay?"

"Oh, yeah. Don't worry about that. It's all taken care of. All I want you to do is be by my side as we get through this ordeal that we are going through."

"Whose car did you drive here?" I asked.

"It's a rental. I got it yesterday. I knew I was going to surprise you with my visit. I do have to take it back tomorrow, though. I got to get back to Austin to take care of Michelle and Tyrone. I'm not letting them get away with anything."

"I'm so tired, Charles," I said, entering the passenger's side.

"I know my Love; I'm tired too. I just want all this shit to be over." Charles slid in the driver's seat and cranked the car.

The car hummed as he put it in reverse. Jill Scott was preaching through the speakers with her lovely voice. I then thought about what Charles told me.

"Charles, you are not going to stay longer?" I could tell Charles was not looking forward to this question, for he made a face as if he controlled the steering wheel.

"No, Samone. I won't be able to stay longer. I know you want me to stay longer, but we need to get our lives back. I can't take this no more. Michelle and Tyrone are at making trouble and I have to stop them.

"You know Captain Haynes is trying to make trouble for you, right?"

"Who told you that, Samone?"

"Dedra told me she had a conversation with him. I'm not sure what he has planned but be careful, Baby." Charles sat in silence, taking in what I just spilled out to him. I interrupted his train of thought with a question.

"Baby, where are we going?"

"I thought I would take you out shopping to get your mind off of things. I know you may need some things back at the cabin."

Charles was such a thoughtful and loving man; I see why I want to keep him in my life. We rode in silence, but the radio spoke for us. I was so glad to get out of that cabin. Charles was right on time by coming to visit me. I needed it. I needed to see his face and have his voice make my body react. He knew just what to do too. The drive was nice, just being in Charles's presence made all the difference in the world. I knew he wanted to protect me from all the evils and misfortunes that seemed to come my way.

I forgot how far the cabin is from town. It took us 45 minutes just to make it to Walmart. I had a love and hate thing for Walmart. I loved the fact that you could find just about anything in the store, but you have to pay a cost by waiting in line and parking. Every Walmart that I have entered always had a large amount of people, but I had to suck it up and go inside. "What do you need out of here, Sweetheart?" Charles soothingly asked. I began to calculate a list in my mind. There wasn't really anything I needed, but what woman would resist her man taking her shopping?

"I need some food, some feminine products, and some clothes."

Charles took my hand while we walked into the store. He squeezed it to reassure me that I was his lady and no one else could have me. At that moment, I began to wonder if Brian was an affectionate man. I exhaled and that alarmed Charles.

"What's wrong, Baby?"

"Oh, nothing," I lied.

I couldn't bear the thought of him knowing the truth. It was heavy on my heart to just tell the truth, but I began to think why I should do that. Charles's phone rang and he took it from his back pocket.

"Who is that?" I asked.

"Captain Haynes," he answered. Charles took the call and could tell he didn't like what he was hearing.

"Captain, I'm not sure where you heard this information, but I have nothing to do with that. Yes, I can come in tomorrow. No, I haven't heard from Ms. Gray. Alright. Thanks. Bye." He ended the call and looked at me.

"Samone, I think I may have to camp out with you." All kinds of thoughts began to come like rushing water.

"Why do you say that, Charles?" He could see that I was serious because he then became serious.

"Loosen up, Samone," he laughed. I then realized that he was only joking with me.

"You are so mean, Charles." He then swallowed me with his arms.

"I mean it. I thought something bad happened."

"It did," Charles said.

"What happened?"

"The Captain just informed me that he received an anonymous letter from someone. The letter said that I was involved with the fire of Joshua's mansion. I'm not sure if I want to go, but if I don't, I know he will put out a warrant for my arrest."

"He can't do that, Charles. He has nothing on you. Captain Haynes is just desperate to make an arrest. He is trying everything in his power to put either you or myself in jail."

"That's why I'm going to meet up with him. I want him to know I have nothing to hide."

We walked around the store and grabbed a couple of items and food. He told me that the Captain would not be able to trap him into telling the secret truths regarding Joshua. He reassured me that I would be fine, but it wasn't I that I was concerned about. I wanted Charles to come home to me every night.

Then out of nowhere, Charles asked me a question, "…have you heard from Brian?"

My heart skipped a beat. I stumbled for words to say, but I hurried and gained my composer. I thought for a second to lie, but then I had second thoughts.

"Yes, I've spoken with him."

"Oh yeah? That's good. What did he have to say?"

"Uh oh, I was in trouble," I thought to myself. I couldn't tell him the truth about the conversation that we had.

"Oh, he just said that he was still working on my case and that I have nothing to worry about."

"Well, I believe him. He's a good guy and he's good at what he does."

Charles paid for my things after we waited in line for 10 minutes.

I thought to myself... *"he wouldn't say that if he knew what Brian was up to."*

"Yeah, he is a good guy. He didn't have to get us out of jail, but he did."

"Yeah, I couldn't believe that. It made me wonder, though," Charles announced.

"What have you been wondering?" We were now in the car, headed to another destination.

"Well, to be honest... I don't get why he bailed me out. I know why he bailed you out."

"Oh really? Why is that?"

"Samone, com' on now. You know that man likes you." There was a split second of silence before I interrupted it.

"Well, he may like me, but I'm with you. I know who I want and it ain't him." I had a feeling something was about to go down. Charles became really quiet as if he were studying my words.

"Did you enjoy that kiss?"

"Charles, how could you ask me something like that? I thought we squashed this."

"It's just a question, Samone."

"You already know the answer, Charles," I said out of disgust.

"No, I don't know Samone. That's why I asked you. So, did you enjoy it?" I did not want to answer the question. The fact is, I did enjoy it.

"Do you want the truth? No, I didn't. It was something that just happened. There! Are you happy?"

"Yeah, Samone. I'm happy."

"Don't be so sarcastic." Charles didn't say anything else until we pulled up to a house.

I didn't recognize who lived here, so I asked, "Who lives here?" Charles turned the car off and got out of the car.

I couldn't believe he still felt some sort of way about the kiss. I sat in the car until I realized Charles was waiting for me. I got out of the car and walked over to where he was standing.

"Look, Samone, before we enter into this house, I want you to know that kiss doesn't mean anything to me. You told me what happened and I believe you." As Charles was speaking, a woman who looked to be in her fifties opened the front door.

"Charlie! Hey Baby, it's good to see you. Come here."

Charles turned his attention to the woman and said, "Hey, Mama. It's good to see you too!"

He left my side and engulfed his mother with a big bear hug. They hugged for a while as if they hadn't seen each other in a long time. It made me smile. I had never met Charles's mother before. So, Charles surprised me with this one. I was taken back because he looked just like his mother, except she was darker.

"And who is this beautiful young lady?" I stood there smiling and waiting for an introduction.

Charles's mother's hair was styled with locks. Her face was nice and round. She was a plumped woman who carried her weight well. Her brown eyes looked to be full of compassion and wisdom.

"Mama, I want you to meet the love of my life, Samone." I extended my hand to shake hers, but she dismissed it with a hug. Just as I was about to say something, Chico's dad joined us.

"Hey, Charlie! How are you doing?"

"I'm doing good. How about you, Ray?"

"Ah, I'm okay. Have you heard the latest on Chico?" Charles's jaw twitched. I guess he didn't really want to talk about it.

"No, I haven't. I've been with Samone." Ray turned his attention to me.

"Oh. I didn't know you had someone special." Ray stood 6'3. He had a lean body and his complexion was as if he had a natural tan.

"Yeah. I thought I would bring her by and introduce her to you guys."

"Well, come on in," his mother said.

We all entered the house and planted ourselves in the living room. I was so surprised by the visit that I just sat quietly. Charles's parents had a lovely home. The living room consisted of rose and olive green. The sectional was nice and comfortable. The coffee and end tables were made of cherry oak and a nice stained marble. Charles's parents loved plants and flowers. Although most of them were phony, they were well cared for. There was a china cabinet with pictures of baby Charles and Chico. It was nice china as well. I went over to take a look at the pictures. I never saw any pictures of Charles when he was younger or a baby, for that matter. He was so adorable. One picture had both Charles and Chico standing together.

"That's my son right there," Ray chimed.

"Charlie. Who is this young lady? You didn't even introduce us," Charles's mother exclaimed.

"Oh, I'm so sorry. Mom and Ray, this is Samone. My fiancé. Samone, this is my mother Charlotte and my stepdad Ray."

We all shook hands and set down on the sectional, all except Ray, who sat in a chair. Charles took my hand and squeezed it. I didn't know how to feel about the whole thing. I felt Charles should have introduced me to his family with me knowing about it.

"Fiancé? I tell you the truth Ray, these kids," Charlotte exclaimed.

"I know Honey. They don't tell us anything." Ray got up from the chair and went into the other room.

"Fiancé? Charlie, why haven't you brought this young lady around before? And when are you two getting married? You two have a lot to explain. Frankly, I don't know if I should be upset or happy."

"Mama, I'm sorry this was just sprung up on you this way. But there is no way you should be upset. Samone and I are getting married soon. We haven't quite set a date." Charles looked over at me and I smiled.

There was no way I was about to Charles's mother why were not sure of the date. The only thing I could come up with is the fact that we are both in trouble. My mind began to wonder about the fact that Charles had to go and face Captain Haynes by himself. I didn't want him to go alone, but I knew Charles wouldn't hear of me going after what happened at Joshua's. Charles' mother gleamed at the both of us staring at each other.

"Me and Ray still stare at each other like the way you two are," Charlotte broke the silence. I looked away from the dreaming eyes of Charles. Charles smiled.

"What did you say Mama?"

"She said, her and Ray still stare at each other as the way we were." Charlotte let out a little giggle.

"I thought she didn't have a voice there for a moment." I looked over at Charlotte to find her staring down the hall for her love Ray.

"You two stay here. I have to go and check on Ray."

"Ah Mama, you know he hates that. Just chill here with us." I guess Ray heard the conversation.

"I'm coming. I just wanted to share something with you before you decide to get married."

Charles stood silent. I could tell he was wondering what Ray could possibly have to share. Ray came out with a medal from what looked like the Air force.

"I wanted to give this to Chico, but he is too young to understand about it. Here take it and I will tell you why you should think about marriage."

"First of all, Ray, that's Chico's birthright. I can't take it. Chico would never forgive me. Second, what does this medal have to do with marriage?" I wondered the same thing Charles did. Ray had his arm extended with the medal in his hand.

"Please take this. Chico will get over his anger. I want this medal to stay safe."

"Ray, you just don't understand. Chico does know about that medal and he wants it. I remember as kids, you would tell us about how long it's been in the family. Chico told me it belonged to your father's father." Ray beamed with satisfaction.

"Chico told you that?"

"Yes, Ray. He knows more than you know." Ray closed his palm and put his arm by his side.

"Thanks for being honest and not letting me make a mistake. You are right; Chico would be upset."

Charlotte hugged Ray and said, "Oh my goodness, Ray, you were going to give that to my son. I love you for thinking of him."

Ray took Charles' mother in his arms and told her in Spanish I love you. I could tell that medal meant a lot to Ray. I stood there looking at Ray and Charlotte embracing each other. I then turned my attention to Charles. Charles had a little smile on his face. It looked as if he had accumulated tears in his eyes. Charles saw me looking at him and he shielded his face from me and wiped away the accumulated tears.

"Samone, I think it's time for us to go. You know we have the thing to go to," Charles said. I didn't know what thing we had to do, but I played along.

"Oh yeah, Charles, you are right. We do." Charles and I both turned our attention to Ray and Charlotte.

"Oh, Baby, you just got here. You don't have to leave so soon," Charlotte exclaimed.

"Well, I thought I would bring my future wife by to meet my beautiful mother and wonderful father." Both Charlotte and Ray looked at each other to reassure each other that Charles would be back.

"Well, it was nice meeting you, Samone and don't become a stranger."

I smiled and replied, "as long as you will have me. It was nice meeting the both of you."

"Likewise," Charlotte said.

Charles took me by the hand and led me to the door. I had no clue where we were headed to next, but I was in for the ride.

"Charles, where are we going now, I whispered?" Charles didn't respond. He opened the door and motioned for me to exit.

"Okay, Son. I want you to come back and visit me again." We were walking to the car when Charles yelled back to his mom that he loved her and that he would be back.

As soon as we were in the car, I asked Charles again where we were going.

Slightly irritated, he responded, "We are on our way to see Chico. I haven't seen him since I've been with you and he has been asking about you, so that's where we are off to." Charles cranked up the car and it began to hum.

I began to think about how he introduced me to his mother as a surprise. I guess he didn't want me to get too nervous thinking about it. I was happy he introduced me to her and Ray. Now I know more about him and where he comes from. We took down the road and headed toward the hospital. We were traveling at about 70 miles per hour when my phone rang.

"Hello. Who is this?" There was just breathing on the other end of the phone.

"Hello," I said again. Again no one said anything. I hung up the phone.

"Who was that?" Charles asked.

"I don't know. There was just silence."

"Well, it's probably a bill collector." I thought about what Charles said. Yeah, maybe he was right. Maybe it was a bill collector.

"What if it's Tyrone?" Charles's facial expression changed from an innocent face to an enraged expression.

"It better not be him if he knows what's good for him. I already took care of his boss. He really shouldn't underestimate me." I could tell Charles was bothered by the whole idea of it being Tyrone so, I tried to change the subject.

"Your mother is so sweet."

"Samone, I swear if that man gets close to you..." His words faded and became void.

"Charles, I should be safe. No one knows where I am except Dedra."

We finally made it to the hospital and it seemed to be very busy, but I guess it was not no more busier than usual. When we made it to Chico's room, people were standing outside his door, just hanging out.

"Aww, look who it is, the man himself. The man with the master plan."

I knew Charles heard one of Chico's homeboys ranting to him, but he didn't say a word just as we were about to enter the room, the same man that was ranting blocked Charles and my way.

"Could you please step aside?" Charles asked. "I know you hear me talking to you."

"Yeah, I heard you. So what?" The young man looked over Charles to see if he could take him.

Charles didn't back down from the fight. The young man stepped aside and we entered the room. When we entered the room, Charles was talking to some of his friends and in good spirits.

"Awww, hol' up. There he is. My brother and his lovely girl."

"Hey, Chico! Are you doing better?" I readily asked. Charles hugged Chico from the bed.

"It's good to see you, Man."

"Thanks for comin' by and bringin' Samone." Chico turned his attention back to me and smiled.

"Samone. Wat' you been up to? You still know how to shoot?" He laughed to himself as if he was a comedian.

"Ah, Chico. I've been okay considering all the trouble I'm in."

"Well, don't let it get you down, Queen. And I'm okay."

"What's going on Chico? You having a party right now?" Charles asked.

"Why you say dat' Bro?"

"It looks like everybody and they mama outside and in here visiting you today.

Chico smiled a huge smile and said, "Yea, I do feel special today. It feels nice."

"Hey Chico, do you know when you getting out of here?" one of his homeboys asked.

We all turned our attention to the young thug that was standing by a window. He looked to be in his early 20s. He had locks that were to his shoulders and he wore jeans and a t-shirt.

"Ah. I'm sorry. I didn't mean to interrupt." The young thug, who I later learned was Kevin, turned his attention back out the window.

"Naw Man. You cool. I would like to know the same thing," Charles said.

"Well, the doc said I may be in here two mo' weeks. I'm tired of lying on my ass. I'm ready to get out of this bed."

"I know you are Chico, but it's doctors' orders," I said. Chico turned his head to face me.

"Samone, you can save that language for somebody else. I don't want to hear that." I didn't respond.

"Where you two coming from?" Chico asked.

"From mom's house." Chico smiled.

"Did you see my dad?"

"Yes. I did. They are doing good too. They miss you. When was the last time you seen them?" Chico looked from Kevin to Charles, then me.

"Aw. They haven't been up here to see me yet." Charles's facial expression turned angry.

"What do you mean they haven't been up here?"

"Charles, I don't want to talk about it right now."

"I can't believe it. They didn't say one word," Charles spat out.

I could only imagine the hurt Chico must have felt. His own father and stepmother hadn't made it to the hospital to visit him.

"Excuse me, but you all are going to have to leave."

"What? Why?" I could hear the conversation going on outside Chico's door.

The nurse came in and told us that we were going to have to leave. Only the immediate family could stay. Chico was vexed by this new order. One of Chico's friends followed the nurse in the room.

"Why do we have to leave nurse?" he asked.

"It's the doctor's orders, not mine. I'm just relaying a message."

The nurse left the room after she checked the monitors for Chico's vital signs. All of Chico's friends began to tell him bye and that they would see him later.

"See you later, Chico," Kevin waved.

"Later Homes." Kevin left his room as well as his other friends.

"Are y'all about to leave too?"

"Nah, I wasn't planning on it," Charles said with a smile. Both Charles and I took a seat.

"So, tell me, Bro. How did that meeting go?" Charles shied.

"I can't get into all that right now, Chico. We are at a hospital and no, I don't know if we are being bugged or what."

"Well, I'm waiting on you. I have a surprise for you when I get out of here."

While Charles and Chico had their own conversation, my mind began to drift. I began to think about Lena. She wasn't around and she was usually by Chico side.

"Chico, where is Lena?" Both men were laughing and I caught Chico off guard.

"Lena?" Chico said, surprised.

"Yes, Chico. Lena." The room was became very silent and I waited for the answer.

Chico exhaled before he told me, "She went somewhere for me."

"Where?" Charles asked?

"I can't tell you that, or I will ruin the surprise."

"Well, is she safe? Is she in any danger?"

"Samone, chill. Lena knows how to take care of herself." I looked at Charles, who was satisfied with Chico's answer.

"Well, Bro, if you not going to tell me, then I'll just have to wait."

"Yup! You are cuz' I'm not tellin' you anything."

Hours passed by and visiting hours were over. It was time to go.

"Bro, I'm going to talk to ma and pa about visiting you. They shouldn't be leaving you in here along like that."

"They'll come when they ready. Y'all come back to see me, okay?" We both stood and gave a hug to Chico.

"Today was a good day, Chico."

"Yes, it was Samone."

Both Charles and I left Chico lying in bed watching TV. It was good seeing him in good spirits. Time flew by and my stomach was talking to me.

"Can we get something to eat, Baby?"

"Yeah, I'm hungry too," Charles announced.

We stopped at a local Whataburger and ate indoors. The food was delicious, or maybe I was only hungry.

"Charles, do you think I can go back home now? I've been stuck in that cabin for a while now and I'm ready to go.

"Out of the question. You're safe and no one knows your whereabouts." I gave him the puppy dog eyes; it didn't work.

"Samone. I don't care what you think; you're safe and you are not going to change that by leaving the cabin." I became silent. I didn't know what to say to make him change his mind.

When we finished our meals, we headed to the car and my phone rang. I looked at the number and I didn't recognize it.

"Hello." All I heard was someone breathing, so; I hung up the phone. At first, the random calls didn't make me sweat, but now I'm getting worried.

I really didn't want to tell Charles about the calls but, I decided to tell him, "Charles, I keep getting random calls from someone who just breaths on the phone." Charles looked at me with a concerned look.

"Samone, we have to get you back to the cabin. I don't know what made me take you with me." Charles shook his head in shame.

"No, Charles, you didn't make a mistake in taking me with you. I wanted to get out of that cabin." I waited for Charles to respond.

"Baby, I'm going to take care of that person who keep calling you. Don't worry."

I could care less about those phone calls right now. Charles was taking me back to that cabin! Those calls did get me to thinking, though. *"Who was it, I wondered? Why did they keep calling me,* I asked myself?"

"It's probably Michelle and Tyrone, Charles."

"Yeah, you right. It's probably them, which reminds me I have to take care of those two."

The thought of Tyrone and Michelle spooked me out. They were young, vicious, and free. They could be doing anything right now. I let Charles be the last to respond.

After 30 minutes, we were back at the cabin. When we made it to the door, I found a note. Charles snatched the note from my hand.

"Who knows you are here, Samone," he asked? After reading the note and realizing it was only my dad, he handed the note to me.

"So, you back in touch with your dad now?" Charles hesitatingly asked. Charles didn't know much about my dad, so he was surprised to see he had left a note.

"Yes. We are on speaking terms right now."

"Do your mom know?" I read the note and folded it back up.

"Yes, my mom knows. I told her about it."

I opened the door to the cabin and let myself in. Charles followed and shut the door. I found my favorite sitting spot on the sofa and set down. Charles was still standing and rubbing his hands together.

"Take a seat here next to me, Baby. I won't bite." I laughed a little.

Charles sat next to me and asked, "How long has he known you are here." I really didn't feel like being interrogated, but this was new for

Charles and I understood the questions.

"I mentioned that I was here about a few weeks ago. I'm surprised to find that he has been here."

"Yeah. It may be a good thing, though. Maybe he can check in on you when I leave," Charles suggested.

"Yeah, maybe so," I agreed.

"Well, Samone, I have to get going. I have to find out what's going on and why you keep getting random calls."

"Oh no, Baby, don't leave me. I don't want to be here alone again." I stood up to hide my face, but Charles stood and embraced me in his arms. I let the tears go and his shirt was becoming wet.

"I know you hate it here, but you being here is the best load of my shoulders. I know you are safe. You know what I mean?"

Dimples put just enough space between us that he lifted my head and looked within my eyes. He kissed me and we made love before he left me alone again. I hated to see him drive off right before sunset. I was glad that he gave me a nice memory. I was out of the shower by the time I heard my phone ring and it was my sister. It was nice to hear the sound of my sister's voice. She sounded excited about something and it seemed she wanted me to be excited for her.

"Hello! Hey Samone. How are you doing in that cabin?" I knew my sister felt my pain of being alone, but she was way too excited about something than to let my misfortunes hurt her.

"I'm okay, Sis. I'm just ready to get on with my life with Charles."

"Charles, huh?" she asked.

Before I could answer, she interrupted and said, "what have you been doing in that cabin since I last left you?" My sister had interrupted me to ask me another question; however, I allowed myself time to reply.

"Dedra, what's up with you? Why are you so everywhere with your questions?" I asked my sister.

"Oh, Girl, I've just been missing you around here with me. Maybe you can come back and live with me here in the city."

"Are you crazy Girl, Charles would kill me."

"Charles, huh?"

"Yes, Dedra. Charles. To tell you the truth, I just met Charles's parents." I was so excited on the inside. I knew in my heart I had a man that wanted me for me.

"Well, if that's who you want..."

"Dedra, you say that as if you know something about Charles that I don't. Is there something?"

Dedra hesitated on the phone for a second. After scuffing along some words, she said, "Honey, your man is asking and doing too many things here. That reporter from the news keep calling me. Janet something, my sister thought out loud."

"That's Michelle's sister," I interrupted.

"Really? I didn't know that," Dedra said.

"Yes. Sis, she was trying to get information out of me recently too. When I was in Austin, we talked."

"What did you talk about?"

"I'm not about to discuss that over the phone. I don't trust this. You know Captain Haynes is looking for us. Why are you asking me to come home?"

"No reason, but I miss you." I could hear it in her voice that she was telling the truth.

"I miss you too, Sis, I really do. I wish I could come there and live with you for a while, but that would be suicide with what's going on. I have to look out for Charles and me right now. And that is what's important to me. Maybe you can come and visit me here?"

"Is Charles there with you?!" she snapped.

"Uh no, Sis. He is not here and why are you snapping on me?"

"Because he is not there with you. He should be there in hiding with you instead of running the streets."

I could tell I was getting irritated. She was pushing all the buttons to get me upset. I loved Charles and I wasn't going to let anyone talk bad about him.

"Samone. It seems like Charles is in a world of his own, you feel me?"

"No, I don't feel you."

Although I knew the truth hurt and I hated to hear it, she was right. Charles did act mysterious on some things I asked him. All of a sudden, I hated Charles left. When I was about to interrupt the silence that came between us, she beat me to it.

"Samone, I'm only concerned about your safety. I mean, have you met his family. Have he at least came to visit you?"

"Yes to all of your questions. I met his mom and stepdad. I'm just waiting to clear my name and he is helping me do that, Dedra. Why do you hate him so much now?"

"I'm sorry. I guess he is being genuine, but he needs to be a bit more attentive to you."

"Don't worry Sis, Charles is treating me good and I love him. He makes me feel safe and I think he is a wonderful protector." There was another awkward moment of silence. I was about to speak when another call came through on my phone.

"Hold on, Dedra, someone is calling me. Hello..."

There was silence on the phone. No one was speaking, just breathing on the phone. I was about to hang up the call when I heard Brian's voice.

"Samone. How are you?" I was startled to hear Brian's voice.

"Brian. Is that you?"

"Yes, Samone, how are you?" He repeated himself and I could tell something was wrong.

"Look, Brian, I have my sister on the other end. Call me back later." Brian mumbled something under his breath before he agreed.

"What did you say?"

"Oh, nothing, only I want to see you. It's important." I hadn't told Brain where I was, and at the moment, I didn't trust no one to know where I was.

"Brian, I don't think that's a good idea you coming here. Maybe when the air is clear and I can breathe again, we can see each other. Until then, I think it's a good idea for us to just speak to each other."

"You don't understand, Samone. It's important that I see you. I can't tell you what I have to over the phone."

I forgot I had my sister on the other end and I clicked over to tell her I would call her back, but she had already hung up. I clicked back to Brian to find him waiting patiently.

"Brian, what's going on. What is so important that you have to see me?"

"Well, I will fill you in a little bit. It's about Joshua's money." I began to think about Joshua. Just hearing his name made goosebumps chill my body.

"Joshua's money. Why do you need to see me about that? I don't have a clue."

"Samone, the money is gone." When I heard that news, it made my knees weak and I had to sit down.

"What do you mean it's gone?"

"Just what I said. It's gone. Now Captain Haynes is investigating the issue. You know he has it out for you, right?"

"Yeah. I know. He has a grudge against me."

"Well, if it makes you feel any better, the Captain has other suspects in line to investigate."

"Charles. Can I change the subject and ask you a question?"

"Charles? I'm not Charles Samone. I'm Brian. Charles is not here to help you like I can. What can he do?" I could hear the self-confidence in his voice. Brian kept gloating and it began to get under my skin.

"Okay, Brian. I get it. You are a lawyer with a well-deserved reputation, but you don't have to rub it in my face."

"Samone, are you going to let me come see you?"

"Let me think about it first."

"Don't think too long and hard because this is important and it needs attention right away."

"I won't; I will let you know something tomorrow.

CHAPTER NINE

Brian set across from me at the kitchen table.

"I've been doing some digging of my own and I have found out that Joshua had a guy named Tyrone do his dirty work." I found Brian to be a very crafty man to dig up things I already knew. He could have asked me, but he didn't.

"Yeah, Tyrone and Joshua were good friends."

"Oh, so you know Tyrone?" I hesitated before answering.

"Yes, we use to all hang out. Tyrone was Joshua's number one man." Brian studied me over to make sure I was telling the truth.

"Well, Samone, I need you to describe Tyrone to me. Because he could have been the one to take the money." I looked away from his eyes and mumbled, I doubt it.

"What was that, Samone? You have something you want to say?"

I faced him and said, "I said I doubt that."

"Do you know something I don't know, Samone? I know you do, for you and Joshua were involved with each other." I pretended I didn't hear his question.

"Brain, what does the money have to do with me?"

"Samone. Stop playing games and tell me who took the money?"

"I don't know what you are talking about. I don't know who took Joshua's money."

"With all the digging I did, you want to know what else I found out?" I could sense Brian knew that I knew more than I was telling. "I found out before Joshua died he left the keys and banking information to you. So, again who took Joshua's money?" I was beginning to regret letting Brain come over. We sat in silence for about two minutes, which felt like 10.

"Brain, I'm not going to tell you again that I don't know who took Joshua's money. If you don't believe me, you can leave."

Brian sucked his lips and said, "Okay, Samone. I'll leave you alone, but you can still help me find Tyrone."

"No, I won't help you. He tried to kill me. Don't act stupid, Brian, you know that."

"I'm sorry, Samone, I didn't realize." Silence.

I looked Brian over like it was my first time meeting him. He still had a handsome face and the suit to match it.

"Well, Samone, I'm not sure how much more I can help you if you are not willing to talk. I'm trying to help you. I don't want to see you doing 5 to 10 in prison." I smacked my lips to let him know that I wasn't falling for his mouthpiece.

"Brian, everything I know, you know. If it's nothing else, you can leave. I won't be interrogated or be in an interview concerning Joshua's money."

Brian picked up his cell phone and keys. To my surprise, he was leaving. I stood from the table and Brian looked me over. I could tell what he was thinking.

"Are you leaving now?"

"Yes. I think that is the best idea." Brian towered over me and waited to embrace me.

"Samone, if you need anything or if you hear from Tyrone, would you please call me?"

His eyes pleaded with me and with no hesitation, I answered him with, "Yes, I will." We hugged, then Brian leaned in to kiss me; I turned my head.

"No, Brian, none of that."

"Okay."

A few months ago, I would have kissed him, but I was serious about my commitment to Charles. I followed Brian to the door. He turned around and told me that he would be waiting on my call.

"Okay, Brian. I will see and talk to you later." He was gone.

After my shower, my stomach started to talk to me. The need the satisfy my hunger it was unbearable. In the refrigerator was full of breakfast food and microwave dinners. I had canned goods, a bag of potatoes, snacks, and box dinners. I figured I would let Charles know that it was time to go grocery shopping. After five minutes of looking into the refrigerator, I grabbed a dinner from the freezer. It wasn't what I really wanted, but it was the best choice for the moment. While my dinner was in the microwave, I went into the living room and flicked on the television. To my surprise, it was Captain Haynes on the tube. I turned up the volume so that I may discover what the news was.

"Today, I'm asking every Texan to be on the lookout for a local killer. He or she is considered armed and dangerous. This case has been on my desk for a couple of weeks and the perpetrator will not get away with this."

Captain Haynes kept my attention and when a commercial appeared, I clicked the television off. My mind began to wonder who was Captain Haynes looking for? I wasn't sure if he meant Charles and I or someone totally different. The microwave alarmed me with its beeping; it was time to eat. Aft finishing my meal, I began to scroll through my phone. Who could I call? I was bored and I wanted to visit my friends.

I began to think about my job and supervisor. I knew I couldn't go back, for it had been too long. My appointment to see my psychiatrist had been passed. I missed the appointment being stuck at this cabin. I selected Dr. Givins's number and the phone began to ring.

"Good afternoon. You have reached Dr. Rene Givins's office; how may I help you?" The voice on the other end sounded cheerful and full of life.

"Yes. I would like to speak to Dr. Givins, please."

"Who may I say is calling?" she asked.

"You can tell her Samone Gray would like to speak to her."

"Sure thing! May I put you on hold for a minute?"

"Sure." The secretary put me on hold and I began to hear the jazz music play. I waited for about five minutes when I heard Dr. Givins voice.

"Hello, Ms. Gray. You missed your appointment last month. How is the medication working?" Dr. Givins was straight to the point and I liked it.

"The medication is fine and I called to set up another appointment with you."

"Ms. Gray, you do realize you need to make your appointments with me so that you can be a healthy-minded individual, right?"

"I'm sorry I didn't make my appointment, but a lot of things have been going on. I know it's important for me to make my appointments and I will make future appointments."

I assumed she was satisfied with my explanation because she said, "Ms. Gray, I hope everything is alright with you and I will go ahead and make you another appointment to see me at the end of this month. Is that okay?"

I thought to myself, *"If I would be able to make in the midst of everything that is going on."*

"Yeah, I should make it."

"Ms. Gray, you don't sound so sure. I would hate to set this appointment up and you not show."

"Yes, Dr. Givins, I will make it. Dr. Givins, could you send another prescription to the pharmacy?"

"Sure. I'll be glad to."

"Thank you."

"Is there anything else I can do for you today, Ms. Gray?"

"No. That's it."

"Alright then, I will see you at the end of the month on the 23rd."

"Okay. I'll see you then." With that, the call ended. That was one thing I could mark off my list of things to do.

I was down to five pills and I knew I had to get that prescription. I wasn't sure how I was going to get it, but I knew I had to. I looked up Charles's number and selected it. The phone rang six times. No answer. *"Where was Charles? And what was he doing,"* I thought. I sat there in silence. No television, no music, nothing. That ended when my phone rang in my hand. The caller ID said caller unknown. Usually, I didn't answer calls such as these, but I did...

"Hello." On the other end, I heard breathing, so I knew someone was just being an asshole.

"Hello," I repeated.

"Samone," they finally said.

I didn't recognize the voice, so I asked, "Who is this?"

"Janice Calbright. I need to talk to you about Michelle." I hadn't heard that name in months, but I knew issues with her were at hand.

"Why did you call me? I haven't heard from Michelle in months."

"Samone, I don't know your whereabouts and I guess that's good. I think Michelle is out to hurt you. So, I would advise you to stay where you are. Don't come back to Austin for a second. Her crazy boyfriend Tyrone is looking for you too. I always thought you were a nice person after the day we met. So, I don't want to see anything happen to you."

"Janice, everything you just explained, I know. That's why I went into hiding. Your sister is crazy."

"Yes. I know she is. I also know what she is capable of. She never was like this until she met Tyrone." Just hearing that name made me cringe.

"Janice, what your sister did to me I can never forgive her of. She is on the hunt to kill me, but she won't succeed. Not to change the subject, but have you been calling my phone and not answer?"

"No. This is the first time I called you in months. Why do you ask?"

"Someone has been calling me and I don't know who it is. I almost didn't answer your call."

"I'm not sure who that could be. Oh My God!"

"What?!"

"I think it may be Michelle or Tyrone."

"I think so too. Do you know where Tyrone and Michelle is right now?"

"Michelle told me that they were going to San Antonio for something; I really don't remember."

"San Antonio, huh?"

"Yes. That's what she said."

"Thanks for that bit of information and I will keep my distance from them."

"Yeah, you do that. I guess I'll talk to you later, Samone."

"Okay. Thanks Janice."

The heat between Tyrone, Michelle, Charles, and I was on. It seemed like everyone was coming out of hiding to tell me what Tyrone and Michelle were up to. All I wanted was for everything to be back to normal, whatever that may be. I wasn't sure how I was going to get out of the situation that I was in. Charles assured me that everything would be okay, but I wasn't so sure. I selected Charles's number and the phone began to ring. No one picked up on the other end. This was beginning to bother me. Whether Charles knew it or not, he worried me. This hasn't happened before and now was not a great time for it to start. I sent Charles a text message hoping he would get back to me. It wasn't long before I got a text message back from Charles it read...

"Sorry Baby, I can't talk right now. I'm in a meeting with the big bosses. I'll chat with you later." I knew what that meant.

Charles stunned me with his ambition to free us from the drug world. I was very relieved to read back from him. It eased my worries, but I became angry. I was pissed at Tyrone and Michelle, Joshua Franks and Captain Haynes. I wanted to see something done about the situation. It was my fault I was in this mess. I should have never gotten involved with a drug lord. I remembered my mother's advice on dating him, she told me...

"Samone, he ain't no good. He will cause you worry and pain. Don't do it Baby. He ain't worth it."

I disregarded her words and replied, "Ah Mama, Joshua is a good man and he loves me. I know what he does ain't the best, but hey, he doesn't involve me."

My mother swore on her father that it wouldn't work. And she was right... it didn't. I've come a long way from that innocent little girl that Joshua knew. Joshua didn't know the fire that I had in me and he wasn't around to see it. I was a good woman to her man... Charles knew it from experience. I respected Charles in whatever he did; I gave him my body. Now, I was willing to make a baby with him. I wanted that fairy-tale love that you read in books, but I wasn't so sure about its accuracy.

Thoughts began to roam and it was nothing I could do about it. I could not break the thoughts. They kept coming fast. Did I take my medication? Was it stress? It wasn't clear what it was, for I remembered taking my medication.

Why was this happening? I cried out, "Help Me God!"

Voices began to appear in my mind. I thought maybe it was God talking to me, but why would he tell me to hurt someone. All my thoughts were about killing or hurting Michelle and Tyrone.

"No, I won't do it!" I screamed.

The voices began to command me to seek out my revenge on them. I wasn't a killer. I barely could kill a bug, let alone a human being. Why were these voices tempting me? Just as I was about to pop a pill, the voices went away. Just like that, I was alone in my thoughts again. What was that, I thought? The thoughts lasted a good 10 minutes before they disappeared. I said a silent prayer to God, and a sense of relief came over me.

It was 8:30 and I wasn't ready for bed. I flicked on the stereo and let the music play. I began to sing along with Johnnie Taylor's last two dollars. It was a nice blues song that I enjoyed to imitate. I checked my phone to see if I had any messages. There was one from Charles. It read, *"Just made it back from San Antonio. See you this weekend."* I was so relieved to have someone come and keep me company. Now all I had to do was wait three days till Saturday. I texted Charles back... telling him about my appointment with Dr. Givins and the pharmacy pickup. He didn't respond right away like he usually did. I hated when he did that. Charles knew I was at this Cabin all alone. He should have taken me with him. Suddenly, I heard a knock on the door. An eerie feeling took over me. I crept to the door as to make no noise.

"Samone. Open the door." The baritone voice was recognizable.

"One second, Dad." I opened the door to find my father grinning from ear to ear.

He was a handsome older man. Samuel stood about 5'11 inches. He had a bald fade haircut with waves; he wore Levi jeans with a white Polo shirt. His smile was white with a few gold teeth in the front. He wore a gold herringbone necklace and a gold bracelet.

"Oh my goodness. Look at you. You are all grown up."

My father stretched out his arms as to welcome me to his embrace. I willingly accepted his invitation. We hugged for a few minutes. When we let each other go, I could see traces of tears on his cheeks.

"Aww... Dad don't cry."

"Samone, you don't know how long I've been waiting to do that. I've missed you and your sister immensely."

I stood there waiting for him to get himself together. He wiped away the tears and followed me in the cabin. When the door was closed, I noticed my father inspecting the room we were in.

"Why didn't you tell me you were coming?"

"I thought I would surprise you."

"When did your flight make it?"

"My flight landed at the airport around fffiivve thirty... I think."

"Oh really? Have you talked to Dedra?"

"No, not yet. I visited friends and colleagues before I came here. I hope that's alright."

"Yeah. Sure. So, how was your flight?" I asked while sitting. My father stood for a few minutes more before he took a seat.

"It was fine, except that crying baby!"

"Where is your wife?" My father seemed startled at the question, for his eyes spoke nervousness.

"She's at home."

"Why didn't you bring her?"

"Well, I didn't know how the both of you would feel about that. I thought I would re-introduce myself first. I didn't want to overbear you two with so much newness." I considered my father's explanation and found it was reasonable.

"And how is my little brother?"

My father let out a little laugh and replied, "He is not so little anymore." I beamed at my dad as he smiled with pride.

"How old is he now?"

"He just turned 21. He has gone off to college on a football scholarship."

"Really? Oh wow! He must be great?"

"Yes, he is. He has made me proud." The smile on my father's face suddenly vanished; he was looking serious, and his tone was even more, "now my mission in life is to make up for lost time with my beautiful daughters if they allow me to."

I didn't know what to say at that moment. Any other daughter would have jumped on the subject and allowed her father to be in her life. I felt horrible after contemplating how my father was there for a young man I had never met; my younger brother, Brice. I thought about how he wasn't there for Dedra or myself. Samuel had given all his love and support to a new family without us.

My father interjected my thoughts, "Samone, you okay? How have things been? I've really missed out on a lot of your life (he took my hand). I do want to apologize right here in person to you. I never meant to hurt you or your sister. I thought it was the best thing to do at the time." I could tell my father was being sincere, but I wanted to make him squirm in his seat.

"No. I haven't been doing that great and things are rough right now." My father's demeanor changed from loving to concern in an instant.

"Is it something I can help you with? I'm here to help you regardless of what it is. I want to build that relationship we once had so long ago. What's going on? You can tell daddy." He gently squeezed my hand.

I thought about telling him the truth, but I didn't know what he would think or do. I didn't want him to freak out and call the cops. Charles was out there trying to clear our names. Charles had texted me that he just made it back from San Antonio... San Antonio... that's where Janice told me Michelle and Tyrone were. Like I said before, I knew what that meant.

My father talked my head off until I couldn't breathe because of laughter. Who knew my father was a comic?

"Just stop," I said, laughing as my hands were waving in the air. He was laughing at his own joke and trying to speak at the same time.

I could only interpret, "Aaahhh... hhhaa... and he said... heee."

"Just stop... ahahaha ooowww hhhaaa." We sat there another 10 minutes laughing with tears in our eyes. It felt great to just sit back and bond with my father.

"Samone, quick pack your things...we have to get out of here. I'm on my way...see you in 45." I read the text from Charles; my nerves were bad and I felt uneasy about the text. Samuel looked at his daughter's face and realized she looked stressed.

"Samone, is everything okay?"

I let the phone drop from my hands to the couch. I looked up and established an expression that took me back to a little girl. It was love, sincerity, and respect in it.

"Dad, I'm in trouble," I bit my bottom lip.

"Uh-huh, what kind of trouble?"

"Trouble, I can't explain right now. Dad, I gotta pack up and go. That's my fiancé Charles who text me."

"Trouble? Go? Wait, Samone, you can't go. I just got here. Sit here and tell me what's going on," he gestured.

"No, Dad, I gotta go. This is something important. This is not like him to text me in the middle of the evening, rushing me along the way."

"Oh wow, Samone. Well, I can't make you stay here. In the meantime, I'll go over a friend's house. I really wish you would tell me what's going on. I'm sure I can help you."

"No, Dad stay out of it," I waived my hands; I walked to the stairs, "look, Dad, I'm sure you know Dedra and I aren't little girls anymore. We have complicated lives that we both share between us. I don't want to disappoint you, buuuutttt... some things are best unsaid." Samuel watched me while I went up the stairs to pack.

It was 9:30; waiting for Charles was exhausting. I threw different items in my bag. I grabbed the rest of my meds...and went downstairs. I found my father pacing the floor and talking to what seemed himself. I followed the voice from the opposite side of the house. My father was easy prey to someone, even myself, for that matter.

"Dad! What are you doing? Are you talking to yourself, too?"

Samuel spun around on his toes and exclaimed, "My Dear, don't scare me like that!"

He clearly allowed me to witness his current phone call. Left-arm up, my dad said it in a little softer tone, "my Dear, please don't scare me like that."

"Yes, Baby, I'm alright. It's only Samone."

"Dad, why are you in the kitchen? And why is panic written all over your face?"

"Samone come here," he beckoned.

"What?"

"Sssshhh Ssshh.... come here. Someone is at the door. From the look of things, I think it's a man." Charles, I thought.

"Why are you so afraid to answer the door dad," I chimed.

"Well, you say you in trouble and I don't know what to expect right now; you can't blame me, Samone." Charles waited for Samone to answer the door and wondered whose car was parked in the front.

"Samone, come open da' door!" I opened the door to find Charles looking like a hot mess.

"Charles, Baby. Is everything okay with you?" Charles slid through the door and made his way to the couch.

"Are you packed and ready to go? We gotta get the hell outta here and fast!" Charles looked consumed with anxiousness as he paced the floor.

"Young man, are you taking my daughter away from the only people she know? Where are you taking her?" Charles and I were both startled by my father.

"Oh Dad, don't worry, I'm in safe hands..."

"No, I don't trust him!"

"Hey Man, you don't even know me. I hate to be meeting you for the first time like this, but we gotta go."

Charles turned his attention and eyes on me, "Go get your things. I'll be in the car waiting and don't keep me waiting too long...cause we gotta get out of here quickly."

"Don't worry, I'll be right out, Baby... but you still haven't told me what's going on?"

"I'll explain in the car; don't worry it ain't nothing I can't handle." Charles slid out the door just like he had entered.

"What's the matter with you, my Beautiful Daughter!" my father cried out, "don't go with him tonight, my Daughter," he continued.

"Dad, I gotta go. Charles has never let me down and I trust him with my life."

"...and that will be just it. Your life," he bravely interrupted.

"Listen, there is no way you are changing my mind, but I just want you to know it's good you came and hung out with me for a while. I'll cherish it wherever I end up. I won't forget you tried to attempt to build some kind of relationship." I turned my back to him to exit the door, but he grabbed a part of my shoulder to turn me around.

"No!" he shouted.

"No, What!? I gotta go," I snapped back. I opened the door and was about to leave when suddenly Charles got out the car.

"Look, Old Man, we got to go now! Don't play no games like you care now. You've never been in the picture and that's the way we gonna keep it. Now go back in the house and call the cops if you want. Samone go get in the car." I jolted back in the present day and hurried to the car.

When I got in, I saw a gun in the back with a huge duffel bag. The zipper was straining to keep the bag closed and it hadn't been successful; I saw money. What did Charles do? Charles was in the car next to Samone in moments. Samone realized she didn't get to say her proper goodbyes to people, especially her father. She didn't know where they were going; she had just jumped in the car, not aware of what was really going on.

"Charles, what did you do?"

"What do you mean, what did I do? I took care of it all, Baby. No more worries. I took care of Michelle and Tyrone dem' asses. It's all done!" he yelled in bliss, "aaaahhh hhaaa it's done, Baby. I took care of it all."

We were flying on I 35 going north. We were headed to Chicago, IL. Charles had filled me in on how he was able to be in on the conversations with the big bosses and Tyrone. The big drug lords were worried about their money invested in Joshua's money laundering scheme. Tyrone was trying to convince them that it was a deal that inclued Joshua and the bosses, not him. They didn't go for it; they wanted their money. At the end of the meeting, both sides had the agreement understood. Tyrone and his crew had to come up with three million dollars.

"Where did that money come from in the backseat?" Charles looked over to me in the passenger's seat, arms folded. A slight smirk appeared upon his face.

"Ah dat'?" Just the way he said it made Samone fume even more.

"Yes, Charles! Where did the money come from? And why are we headed to Chicago?"

Charles exhaled; he was trying to find the right words to explain. When he found that there was not a right way, he blurted out, "It's Tyrone dem' money." Charles sucked his teeth and responded to my silence, "why you get so quiet now? Just a minute ago, you seem like you had plenty to say." When Charles realized I was giving him his moment, he paused and said, "Them fools got what they deserve and there is nothing I can do to bring them back. I have one question for you Samone, are you willing to be my ride or die dime? Because if you are, we can go a long way." I was staring out the window when Charles grabbed my hand. My mind had drifted off and I was in my own thoughts. I hadn't realized he was asking me a question.

"Oh uh. Yeah."

"Samone. I need you to be real with me. Can you handle this situation? I'm sorry I pulled you into something more than you want to be in, but sometimes things just happen."

After hearing the sincerity in his voice, I chose to speak my mind, "Baby, I know you risk your neck out there to try and clear our names, but this shit is deep. I'm down for you, but I don't want to go to prison. I wouldn't make it. Maybe we should just go to the police."

"Hell naw, we ain't going to no cops. I don't want to go to prison either.

You think I want to lose my freedom. Hell to the naw. We got to get this money. Are you with me?" It seemed like Charles had scripted something from a movie and I was uneasy, to say the least.

"Charles, I didn't even get to say bye to him," I whimpered.

"You will get to see him again," Charles assured me.

"Did you see the way he was looking? I just left him without a goodbye." Tears began to fill my eyes. I didn't want to let Charles know the emotions that I held within but hiding it wasn't my forte.

"Baby, are you crying? I told you that you would see him again."

I quickly wiped my tears away and assured Charles I was good. The truth was inside; a war was going on between good and evil. The battle was raging within my mind.

"Charles, we forgot my medication from the pharmacy. I really need to pick that up."

"Don't worry. We can get it transferred."

"...which brings me to the reason of this trip to Chicago? Why are we going there again?"

"Baby Girl, we going to get Joshua's money out that bank. You say you know his account numbers and everything. All you have to do is go in there, show them your ID and take the money. It shouldn't be that hard to do since your name is on the accounts."

"Charles. You are really being greedy right now. You just took that money off of Tyrone and Michelle dem'...let that be that. What if that money was for the bosses... then what? They gonna be after our asses."

"What's up wit you doin' all that cursing? You a'ight?" I assumed he picked up on my irritation. I already had too much going on within and now he was questioning my language?

"Yeah, what about it?"

"Well, you usually do that, so I was just wondering if you were a'ight? We can talk about it, you know?" Samone knew her man was just trying to be helpful, but she wasn't feeling it for some reason.

"I can say what I want when I want, and how I want, and you can't stop me."

"It's like that, Samone?"

I turned my entire body to face him and pushed the side of his head with my index finger, "Yes, it's like that. And for your information, Joshua's money is gone. Someone took it already." Charles sat in anger mixed with confusion; he definitely needed to know what was going on. Who took the money?

"Samone, do you know who took the money?" Charles hesitated to ask.

"Do it look like I know who took that money? Oooh, I'm so tired of people accusing me." We sat in rock cold silence for about an hour. No one said one damn word.

We were still headed to Chicago to see what money we could come up with. I ended up telling Charles about the whole conversation Brian and I shared earlier that day.

By the time the conversation was over, Charles had apologized for asking me about the money. His apology soothed my energy and I told him we should not go to Chicago, but Charles insisted. At that moment, I knew it was more to the story than Charles put on.

"Baby, we can survive off each other. We don't need any more money."

Charles's greed filled his eyes. He somehow knew he was becoming different. The more he got involved, the more he wanted to play the game.

"Look, Samone, I know that Joshua has more accounts than one in Chicago. We are gonna visit all of them. I've planned a busy morning, so get some sleep."

Ms. Gray became exhausted in trying to convince her man differently. So, when he advised her to get some rest, she took him up on it.

I woke up to find we were parked outside of a gas station. I could tell we were in Chicago for the Chicagoans traveled the streets in a rushing manner. A true Chicagoan makes little eye contact and little verbiage when reacting to a southerner's introduction. Charles hurried across the parking lot and bounced in the car. He was still smiling when he looked at Samone.

"Baby, you won't believe that clerk in there. She was so flirtatious; I ended up with everything free except the gas. Ain't that something?"

I felt both good and bad at his last statement. I felt good he was handsome and was with me, but on the other hand, she (the clerk) made him blush like a little schoolboy. Seemed like he loved the attention.

"Maybe I need to go and check that clerk out," I spat out. Charles laughed at the thought.

"Go ahead, my Dear, if you bad a bold." I guess Charles didn't recognize my capabilities of proving my point.

In no time, I was out of the car and headed toward the store. Charles ran up behind me and turned me around.

"Don't worry about her Baby, he wooed, she is not you. I'm in love with you." Dimples made me feel as ease with the explanation. He pulled me in close to him by my waist and gave me a kiss.

"Com' on Baby, let's go back to the car."

I followed Charles back to the car like a lost little puppy. He was my everything; my provider, protector, and friend. I sat in the car waiting for Charles to finish pumping the gas. When he had finished, he told me we could stop somewhere to eat first. I wasn't in the mood for food; all I really wanted to do was lay down. It was early morning, he and I just needed to rest.

"Hey Boo, can we find somewhere to lay down? I'm really tired but not hungry; we can eat later if that's alright?"

"Yeah Baby. We can do that. I'm going to take you to the Drake Hotel. I heard its nice and beautiful. I think you gonna like it," he said.

I was delighted at the thought of a nice fluffy, comfortable, king-sized bed. The Drake Hotel sits off the water in downtown Chicago. Its Gothic building was made of gray stones and huge windows to let in the sun. The building had to be hundreds of years old, if not centuries. I could tell it was a very busy hotel, for even R. Kelly mentioned it in some of his songs. I guess Charles wanted to check it out.

"Well, we are here Baby," Charles announced.

"I can see we are here, Baby it's beautiful." A noticeable upbeat Charles beamed with bliss.

"I'm glad you like it, but let's go in."

I got out of the car and proceeded with Charles through the front doors. Some of the hotel attendants were greeting us as they were trained. When we found ourselves at the front counter where there was a middle-aged woman with red hair, she stood about 5'7 inches. Her perfume was loud, for the smell of it was instantly entered my nostrils.

"Hello and welcome to the Drake Hotel. Do you have a reservation?"

Her thin lips was spread across her face as she gave us a smile.

"No Ma'am, but we would like a room."

"How many nights are you planning to stay? And will there be anyone else joining you?"

As Charles and the woman, Chrissy spoke to one another, I looked over the extravagant hotel. The mixed crowd was so busy getting from one place to the next that they forgot other businesses surrounding them. I saw a young couple with a small child; she had to be about two years old, looking around the hotel as well. Anyone could tell they were foreigners to Chicago. The younger woman of the couple was dressed in a red dress and black 5-inch heels. Her brown locks were to the mid-section of her back. The young woman's eyes met with Samone's; then the young woman waved and smiled. I waved back; I then turned my attention to Charles and Chrissy. Chrissy was handing Charles a key card for the door. Charles thanked the woman and paid the bill in full.

We went to the fourth floor and found a master bedroom, a living area, and a kitchenette for a room. It was enormous and spectacular to say the least.

"Now dis' is what I'm talking bout'," Charles announced. He went from room to room, inspecting our place of rest.

"I'm going to get some sleep Baby," I shared.

"Okay, I'm going to take a shower and then meet you in the bed." I agreed.

The king-sized bed was beyond my expectations. The heavy-duty like white comforter made my restless body relax as I laid down. When I was completely lying in bed, my mind began to race. I wasn't sure why it was happening because I took my medication faithfully. *God if you help me...I won't let you down...*I silently prayed. The more I began to pray the more my mind began to race. Different voices began to sing words of hate and rage in my head. I couldn't concentrate on sleeping if it killed me. I wasn't sure if I was going to get rest or not; so, I got up from bed to go to a chair that held my purse. I took my prescription, opened the lid to find four pills left. I popped one in my mouth and drowned it with a cup of water sitting next to the bed. I climbed back and bed and the medication began to work its magic. The voices seemed to disappear and I was able to focus on sleeping. I was drifting off when Charles told me he was going out for a while. I mumbled a couple of words; he kissed my forehead and Charles was gone off in the day.

"Damn, I hope this money ain't gone yet. I know that loot from Tyrone and Michelle dem' won't last us forever. We got to get this money." Charles exited the elevator and headed out the Drake Hotel. He was glad Samone could get some well-deserved rest. He knew by the end of the day she would need it. Charles had plans to make their life a living bliss. Charles was on Lake Shore Drive on his way to see Chulo Rodriquez. Chulo Rodriquez was a true Chicagoan. He was respected in the common neighborhoods and he was a main character in the streets. Chulo knew of all the drops and where they were going down.

"Hey Man. How you doing," Charles excitedly chimed.

"Aww hey Man. Nutin much Man. You still want to do business?"

"Yeah, I'm on my way."

"But hey Man, I need you to do a drop for me. Nutin in this life is for free. If you still want dem' list of banks den you gonna have to do dis drop for me." Charles knew he didn't want to do the drop. He hadn't done a drop since his teenage years.

"Do you know these dudes Chulo?"

"Yeah Man. I kno dem'. All you hav' to do is, go in and hand dem da money, get the drugs and be out. Dat's it. You got it?"

"Yeah Man I got it. I'll be there in a few to get the money. Have it ready." Charles hung up the phone and pressed the accelerator to move with more speed.

He hadn't realized the beat that was playing through the speakers until he turned the volume up. His favorite rapper was spitting his lyrics when Charles began to recite the words along with the rapper. He felt good and couldn't help but smile at his eerie nonchalant plan to be the next big man in charge.

I woke to find Charles was gone.

"Where could he have gone?" I wondered.

The comforter and bed sheets were soaked with sweat. Samone peeled herself off the layers of warmth and got out of the bed. She searched for her phone to find one missed call. She was about to call her sister back when her phone chimed in her hands.

Charles: Hey Baby! I'm with my man Chulo. I'll be back at the hotel in no time.

Samone: Okay Baby. Hurry up. I don't want to be alone tooo long.

Charles: Okay Baby. Love you!

Samone thought about calling her sister back but opted out. *"I'll call her back later."* She got up from the chair and went into the bathroom. Samone relieved her bladder of the previous day's liquid and then washed her hands. Charles was out taking care of business and she was left alone with thoughts to kill and destroy. Samone could tell that something was taking over her. After all, she had gone through, she was not willing to face her demons.

"This is getting out of control. And now I don't even know if I will make my appointment. I hope I can get my medication filled. I'm down to three pills."

Frustrated at the predicament she was in, Samone left her reflection just where she found it. She picked up the hotel phone and ordered room service. Samone waited on her meal while texting her sister.

Samone: Hey Girl. I'm okay. I'm with Charles.

Samone patiently waited for her sister's response. When she received it she was astonished to read what her sister had to say.

Dedra: Why you leave dad like that? He said you ran off with some dude. Where has Charles taken you?

Samone: Sorry Sis there was no way around it. I had to go. We are in Chicago right now.

Dedra: What?! You gonna wind up in jail running behind Charles.

Samone: Don't say that. We gonna be okay.

Dedra: Keep telling yourself that. You need to leave Charles. Charles is going crazy with the dope game.

Samone just read the texts in silence. She felt unmoved and perhaps glad that Charles was taking care of them. After the next three texts from Dedra, Samone stood to retrieve her meal. She was famished and needed to make her stomach happy again. She knew her sister was not going to let up so she decided not to respond. That wasn't enough for her sister for she called when she didn't receive a text from Samone. Samone ignored the call and began to eat at her food.

"I'll let her cool down first before I call her back."

There was nothing else left to do but lie back in the enormous king-sized bed. Just as she was about to close her eyes, she heard her phone ring. Vexed and irritated at the same time, Samone got up and answered the phone without looking at the caller ID.

"What Dedra?"

"This is not no Damn Dedra Bitch! I know you came to get my money but you won't see the light of day before you do get it. I'm on to you Samone and that no good ass dude you with. Yawl's life is in my hands."

Samone was nervous and scared at the voice she heard on the other end. But could it be true? Was Joshua still alive?

ABOUT THE AUTHOR

In April of 1981, Monica Betts, aka MoniB was born in Little Rock, Arkansas. She later moved to Austin, TX, with her mom and siblings. MoniB has an older sister and is the second eldest of three sisters and four brothers.

Growing up in Austin, Texas, in the ghetto is where MoniB first realized her talent in writing. She would write short stories for school assignments and then be commended on the work. It wasn't until later in life that she realized it was her calling to write.

In 2019, she finished her first manuscript, Love's Mirage. It took much perseverance and dedication to complete the first book of the series.

MoniB now resides in Arlington, Texas, where she writes. She plans to continue writing and give her readers something to talk about for generations to come.

www.ingramcontent.com/pod-product-compliance
Lightning Source LLC
Chambersburg PA
CBHW071432070526
44578CB00001B/87